ALBANIA

TRAVEL GUIDE

2023-2024

The Essence of Albania: A Memorable Travel Guide (2023-2024)

SHEILA J. RYDER

Copyright©2023 by sheila j. Ryder

Allrightsreserved. No part of this publication may be reproduced, distributed, or transmitted in any form or by any means, including photocopying, recording, or other electronic or mechanical methods, without the prior written permission of the publisher

TABLE OF CONTENT

INTRODUCTIONS..................8

Welcome to Albania......................14

About This Guide..........................20

Planning Your Trip........................25

CHAPTER 1

GETTING TO KNOW ALBANIA.............30

History and Culture.....................30

Geography and Climate..............36

Albanian Cuisine..........................40

Language and Communication...................44

CHAPTER 2

PRACTICAL INFORMATION.................49

Visa Requirements..........................49

Currency and Money Matters..................54

Transportation............................58

Getting to Albania........................62

Accommodation Options.....................67

Health and Safety Tips....................73

CHAPTER 3

EXPLORING THE REGIONS................78

Tirana: The Capital City..................78

Local Experiences.........................84

Dining and Nightlife......................88

Northern Albania..........................92

Central Albania...........................96

Southern Albania.........................101

Coastal Riviera..106

Off-the-Beaten-Path Destinations...........111

CHAPTER 4

OUTDOOR ADVENTURES...................116

Hiking and Trekking..................................116

Beaches and Water Sports........................121

Mountain Biking..125

Rafting and Kayaking................................130

Caving...135

CHAPTER 5

CULTURAL EXPERIENCES.................140

Traditional Festivals and Events............140

UNESCO World Heritage Sites.................145

Ottoman and Byzantine Architecture.....149

Traditional Arts and Crafts.....153

Folklore and Music.....158

CHAPTER 6

HIDDEN GEMS AND LOCAL SECRETS.....162

Secret Beaches and Coves.....162

Authentic Local Cuisine.....166

Hidden Mountain Villages.....170

CHAPTER 7

TIPS FOR RESPONSIBLE TRAVEL.....175

Respect for Local Customs and Traditions.175

Sustainable Tourism Practices.....180

Supporting Local Communities.....186

CHAPTER 8

LANGUAGE GUIDE............................191

Basic Albanian Phrases and Expressions..191

APPENDIX...195

Useful Websites and Resources................195

Recommended Reading and Films..........202

Albanian Recipes......................................207

Maps and Transportation Guides............211

INTRODUCTIONS

Albania, a hidden gem nestled in the heart of the Balkan Peninsula, holds a special place in my heart. Its breathtaking landscapes, rich history, and warm-hearted people make it a captivating destination for any traveler seeking an off-the-beaten-path adventure. During my recent visit to this enchanting country, I was fortunate enough to have a truly memorable experience that left an indelible mark on my soul.

My journey began in the capital city of Tirana, a vibrant metropolis brimming with energy and charm. As I strolled through its bustling streets, I was immediately captivated by the kaleidoscope of colors adorning the buildings. Vibrant murals and graffiti art adorned the cityscape, turning every corner into a living gallery. The mix of Ottoman, Italian, and communist-era architecture added to the city's unique character, providing a fascinating glimpse into Albania's complex past.

One of the highlights of my trip was exploring the Albanian Riviera, a pristine stretch of coastline that boasts some of the most beautiful beaches in Europe. The azure waters of the Ionian Sea kissed the white sandy shores, creating a mesmerizing sight. I found myself basking in the sun on the beaches of Saranda, immersing myself in the tranquility and serenity that surrounded me. The locals' warm hospitality and genuine smiles made me feel like I was part of their extended family, creating an atmosphere of pure bliss.

Venturing inland, I embarked on a road trip through the Albanian Alps, an awe-inspiring mountain range that left me breathless at every turn. As I wound my way along the narrow mountain roads, I was rewarded with breathtaking vistas of rugged peaks, deep valleys, and emerald-green lakes. The air was crisp and invigorating, and the silence was broken only by the occasional sound of a distant waterfall. I hiked through dense forests, discovering hidden waterfalls and encountering friendly shepherds tending their flocks. It was a soul-stirring experience that reconnected me with nature in its purest form.

No trip to Albania would be complete without a visit to the UNESCO World Heritage Site of Berat, known as the "City of a Thousand Windows." As I wandered through its cobblestone streets, I marveled at the well-preserved Ottoman-era houses with their characteristic wooden balconies. The ancient castle perched on the hilltop offered a mesmerizing panoramic view of the city below. Exploring the castle's winding alleys and Byzantine churches felt like stepping back in time, unraveling the layers of history that shaped this remarkable place.

One of the most memorable aspects of my journey was the opportunity to savor Albania's delectable cuisine. From the mouthwatering flavors of traditional dishes like Tavë Kosi (baked lamb with yogurt) to the aromatic aroma of freshly brewed Turkish coffee, every meal was a delightful culinary adventure. The locals took great pride in their gastronomic traditions, and I had the pleasure of indulging in farm-to-table meals prepared with locally sourced ingredients. It was a feast for the senses that left me craving for more.

Beyond the natural beauty and cultural wonders, it was the warmth and genuine hospitality of the Albanian people that made my experience truly unforgettable. Everywhere I went, I encountered friendly faces eager to share their stories and traditions. Whether it was the jovial conversations with the locals in the vibrant bazaars or the spontaneous invitations to join in traditional dances at a wedding celebration, I felt a sense of belonging that transcended borders.

Albania, with its mesmerizing landscapes, rich history, and warm-hearted people, has etched a special place in my heart. It was a journey of self-discovery, a chance to explore a country that has emerged from its tumultuous past and embraced its future with open arms. My memorable experience in Albania will forever remain a cherished chapter in my travel memoirs, reminding me of the power of exploration, connection, and the beauty that lies beyond the well-trodden path.

Welcome to Albania

Nestled in the heart of the Balkan Peninsula, Albania is a hidden gem waiting to be discovered. With its rich history, breathtaking landscapes, and warm hospitality, this Mediterranean country offers an unforgettable experience for travelers. Whether you're exploring ancient ruins, relaxing on pristine beaches, or immersing yourself in vibrant city life, Albania has something for everyone.

Albania is known for its diverse and stunning natural beauty. From the rugged mountains of the Albanian Alps to the crystal-clear waters of the Ionian and Adriatic Seas, the country boasts a remarkable variety of landscapes. The Albanian Riviera, with its picturesque coastal villages and secluded beaches, is a paradise for sun-seekers and water sports enthusiasts. The Albanian Alps, on the other hand, offer spectacular hiking trails, where adventurers can explore pristine lakes, cascading waterfalls, and breathtaking vistas.

One of Albania's biggest draws is its rich history and cultural heritage. The country has been inhabited since ancient times and is home to numerous archaeological sites and UNESCO World Heritage Sites. The city of Butrint, located on the southwestern coast, showcases a remarkable fusion of Greek, Roman, and Byzantine ruins. The ancient city of Apollonia, once a center of learning and culture, is a must-visit for history buffs. The medieval town of Berat, also known as the "City of a Thousand Windows," with its well-preserved Ottoman-era architecture, is a UNESCO World Heritage Site that offers a glimpse into the country's past.

Albania's vibrant capital, Tirana, is a thriving city that blends the old with the new. Here, you can explore the lively Blloku neighborhood, once reserved for high-ranking communist officials and now a hub of trendy cafes, boutiques, and restaurants. The city's central square, Skanderbeg Square, is surrounded by historic buildings, including the National History Museum and the Et'hem Bey Mosque. Tirana's bustling markets, such as the colorful Pazari i Ri, offer a chance to experience the local culture and sample traditional Albanian delicacies.

One of the greatest joys of visiting Albania is the warm hospitality of its people. Albanians are renowned for their friendliness and generosity, making visitors feel welcome and at home. Traditional Albanian cuisine, influenced by Mediterranean and Balkan flavors, is a treat for food lovers. Don't miss the opportunity to try mouthwatering dishes such as byrek (a savory pastry), tave kosi (baked lamb with yogurt), and petulla (deep-fried doughnuts). Pair your meal with a glass of locally produced raki or wine for an authentic Albanian dining experience.

For nature enthusiasts, Albania offers a wealth of opportunities to explore its national parks and protected areas. The UNESCO-recognized Albanian Alps National Park is a haven for outdoor activities, including hiking, rock climbing, and skiing during the winter months. The Divjaka-Karavasta National Park, located along the Adriatic coast, is a haven for birdwatchers, with its diverse range of bird species and pristine wetlands.

Albania's affordability also makes it an attractive destination for budget-conscious travelers. Accommodation options range from luxury resorts to cozy guesthouses, ensuring there's something for every traveler's budget. The country's efficient transportation system allows for easy exploration of its various regions, with reliable bus and train services connecting major cities and towns.

As you venture through Albania, you'll discover a country that is full of surprises and contrasts. Its ancient history, breathtaking landscapes, and warm hospitality combine to create a truly memorable experience. Whether you're seeking relaxation on sun-drenched beaches, exploring archaeological wonders, or immersing yourself in vibrant city life, Albania welcomes you with open arms.

Come and explore the wonders of Albania – a land of beauty, history, and adventure that will captivate your heart and leave you with

unforgettable memories.

About This Guide

Welcome to the comprehensive Albania Travel Guide! Whether you are a history enthusiast, a nature lover, or simply seeking an off-the-beaten-path destination, Albania has something to offer for everyone. This guide aims to provide you with all the necessary information to make your trip to Albania an unforgettable experience.

Albania, located in Southeastern Europe, is a hidden gem that has started to gain recognition among travelers in recent years. Known for its stunning landscapes, rich cultural heritage, and warm hospitality, Albania is a destination that offers a unique blend of history, natural beauty, and vibrant traditions.

This travel guide will take you on a journey

through the various aspects of Albania, from its ancient ruins to its pristine beaches, from its charming towns to its rugged mountains. You will discover the country's diverse regions, each with its own distinct character and attractions.

To begin your exploration, the guide provides an overview of Albania's history, tracing its roots back to ancient Illyrian civilizations and its subsequent influences from the Roman, Byzantine, and Ottoman empires. Learn about Albania's struggle for independence and its journey towards becoming a modern European nation.

The guide also delves into Albania's rich cultural heritage, highlighting its traditional music, dance, and folklore. Explore the UNESCO World Heritage Sites scattered across the country, such as the ancient city of Butrint, the historical center of Berat, and the unique Ottoman-era architecture of Gjirokastër.

For nature lovers, Albania offers breathtaking landscapes that range from pristine beaches along the Albanian Riviera to dramatic mountain ranges like the Albanian Alps and the Accursed Mountains. Discover national parks like Valbona and Theth, where you can hike through untouched wilderness and witness stunning alpine scenery.

In addition to the natural beauty, Albania's cities and towns are filled with charm and character. Tirana, the capital city, boasts a vibrant café culture, colorful buildings, and a lively atmosphere. Visit cities like Shkodra, Vlora, and Saranda to experience their unique blend of ancient history and modern development.

Practical information is a crucial part of any travel guide, and this guide has got you covered. From visa requirements to transportation options, from local cuisine to accommodation recommendations, you will find all the essential details needed to plan your trip effectively.

Whether you are a budget traveler or seeking luxury experiences, Albania offers a range of options to suit your preferences. You can indulge in delicious traditional Albanian cuisine, which includes dishes like byrek (savory pastry), tave kosi (baked lamb with yogurt), and rakia (fruit brandy). Discover local crafts and souvenirs in bustling bazaars, or relax on the pristine beaches of the Albanian Riviera.

Albania is a country of contrasts and surprises, where ancient traditions meet modern aspirations. It is a destination that promises to captivate and enchant you with its natural beauty, cultural heritage, and warm hospitality. This travel guide is your key to unlocking the wonders of Albania, helping you create memories that will last a lifetime.

So, pack your bags, embrace the spirit of adventure, and get ready to embark on a journey of discovery in Albania. Let this guide be your trusted companion, providing you with all the information you need to make the most of your visit. Albania awaits you with open arms, ready to offer you an experience like no other.

Planning Your Trip

Planning a trip to Albania offers a unique opportunity to explore a hidden gem in the heart of the Balkans. With its stunning landscapes, rich history, and warm hospitality, Albania has become an increasingly popular destination for travelers seeking an off-the-beaten-path adventure. This guide will provide you with essential information and tips to help you plan a memorable trip to Albania.

Choosing the Best Time to Visit:

Albania enjoys a Mediterranean climate, with hot summers and mild winters. The best time to visit depends on your preferences and the activities you wish to engage in. The summer months (June to August) are ideal for beach lovers, as the coastal regions offer sun-soaked days and vibrant nightlife. Spring (April to May) and autumn (September to October) are great for exploring the countryside, hiking, and enjoying milder temperatures. Winter (December to February) is suitable for skiing enthusiasts, as the Albanian Alps provide excellent opportunities for winter sports.

Must-Visit Destinations:

Tirana: Start your journey in Albania's vibrant capital city, Tirana. Explore the colorful streets, visit the National Historical Museum, and indulge in the local cuisine at traditional restaurants.

Berat: Known as the "City of a Thousand Windows," Berat is a UNESCO World Heritage Site and boasts beautiful Ottoman-era architecture. Explore the well-preserved castle, wander through the narrow cobblestone streets, and admire the panoramic views of the city.

Butrint: Located in the south, Butrint is an ancient archaeological site dating back to the Greeks, Romans, and Byzantines. Explore the well-preserved ruins, including a theater, basilica, and fortifications.

Gjirokastër: Another UNESCO World Heritage Site, Gjirokastër is a captivating city with a rich history and well-preserved Ottoman-era houses. Visit the imposing Gjirokastër Castle, the Ethnographic Museum, and wander through the charming bazaar.

Albanian Riviera: Head to the breathtaking Albanian Riviera along the Ionian Sea for stunning beaches and crystal-clear waters. Explore the beach towns of Saranda, Himara, and Vlora, and don't miss the iconic Ksamil

Islands.

Transportation and Getting Around:

Flights: Tirana International Airport, located just outside the capital, is the main entry point for international travelers. Several airlines offer direct flights to Tirana from major European cities.

Public Transportation: Albania has a reliable and affordable public transportation system, including buses and minibusses that connect major cities and towns. However, be prepared for longer travel times in more remote areas.

Renting a Car: Renting a car is a convenient option to explore Albania, especially if you plan to venture into rural areas. Many international car rental agencies operate in Tirana, and road conditions have significantly improved in recent years.

Accommodation:

Albania offers a wide range of accommodation options to suit every budget. In Tirana and other major cities, you'll find luxury hotels, boutique guesthouses, and budget-friendly hostels. In smaller towns and rural areas, guesthouses and traditional family-run inns, known as "agrotourism," provide an authentic Albanian experience.

Safety and Cultural Etiquette:

Albania is generally a safe country to visit, with friendly locals who welcome tourists. However, like any travel destination, it is important to take precautions and be mindful of your surroundings. Keep your valuables secure, follow local customs and traditions, and be respectful of religious sites.

CHAPTER 1

GETTING TO KNOW ALBANIA

History and Culture

Albania boasts a rich tapestry of history and culture that spans millennia. From its ancient Illyrian roots to the impact of Roman, Byzantine, and Ottoman civilizations, Albania has emerged as a country with a distinct identity shaped by its diverse past. This guide delves into the fascinating history and vibrant culture of Albania, exploring its traditions, architecture, cuisine, and artistic contributions.

Ancient Origins and Illyrian Heritage:

The origins of Albania can be traced back to the ancient Illyrians, an Indo-European people who inhabited the Western Balkans.

Renowned for their warrior culture and skilled craftsmanship, the Illyrians left behind impressive archaeological sites, such as the UNESCO World Heritage site of Butrint. This ancient city showcases the ruins of an Illyrian acropolis, a Roman theater, and a Byzantine basilica, offering a glimpse into Albania's ancient past.

Roman and Byzantine Influence:

During the Roman era, Albania, known as Illyria, became an important province of the empire. Numerous Roman settlements, such as Apollonia, emerged as centers of trade and culture. The ruins of Apollonia still stand today, showcasing magnificent temples, villas, and an impressive theater.

The Byzantine era witnessed the spread of Christianity throughout Albania. Byzantine art and architecture influenced the construction of many churches and monasteries, including the UNESCO-listed Berat and Gjirokastër. These picturesque towns boast a stunning ensemble of Byzantine and Ottoman buildings, with narrow cobbled streets and traditional houses.

Ottoman Legacy:

For nearly five centuries, Albania was under Ottoman rule, leaving a lasting imprint on its culture. Ottoman architecture and customs permeated the country, as seen in the iconic mosques, hammams (bathhouses), and bazaars that still grace the cities of Tirana and Shkodra. The UNESCO-listed city of Berat features a unique fusion of Ottoman, Byzantine, and Albanian architectural styles, earning it the nickname "The City of a Thousand Windows."

National Revival and Independence:

In the 19th century, Albania experienced a cultural awakening known as the National Revival. Intellectuals, writers, and artists played a crucial role in preserving and promoting Albanian language and identity. Notable figures like Naim Frashëri and Ismail Qemali paved the way for the country's independence in 1912, marking a significant turning point in Albanian history.

Rich Cultural Traditions:

Albania's cultural traditions are a testament to its vibrant heritage. The country is renowned for its polyphonic folk music, characterized by harmonies created by multiple voices singing different melodies simultaneously. This unique form of music was recognized by UNESCO as an Intangible

Cultural Heritage of Humanity. Traditional dance, colorful costumes, and intricate handcrafted artwork further enrich Albania's cultural tapestry.

Culinary Delights:

Albanian cuisine reflects the country's geographical diversity and historical influences. From the mountainous regions of the north to the coastal areas in the south, traditional Albanian dishes offer a tantalizing blend of flavors. Iconic dishes include qofte (meatballs), fërgesë (baked cheese and peppers), and byrek (savory pastry). Olive oil, dairy products, and fresh vegetables form the backbone of Albanian gastronomy.

Contemporary Albanian Culture:

Albania has experienced rapid development in recent decades, with a flourishing arts scene and a growing film industry. The National Gallery of Arts in Tirana showcases both classical and contemporary works by Albanian artists, while the Tirana International Film Festival has gained international recognition. The country's vibrant culture continues to evolve and embrace modern influences while honoring its deep-rooted traditions.

Geography and Climate

Albania shares borders with Montenegro, Kosovo, North Macedonia, and Greece. The Adriatic and Ionian Seas flank its western coastline, offering breathtaking views and a Mediterranean climate. Let's explore the geography and climate of Albania in detail.

Geographically, Albania is known for its stunning landscapes, including towering mountains, fertile valleys, and picturesque coastlines. The country is dominated by the Albanian Alps in the north, which form a natural border with Montenegro. The highest peak, Mount Korab, stands at 2,764 meters (9,068 feet) and provides a challenging destination for hikers and mountaineers. Moving south, the terrain transitions into the central mountain range, with peaks like Mount Dajti overlooking the capital city,

Tirana. To the east, the country gradually slopes towards the fertile lowlands and the vast Lake Ohrid, which is shared with North Macedonia.

Albania is blessed with an abundance of rivers and lakes, making it a haven for water enthusiasts. The Vjosa River, known as the "Blue Heart of Europe," flows uninterrupted for 270 kilometers (168 miles), offering thrilling rafting experiences. Lake Shkodra, the largest lake in the Balkans, straddles the border with Montenegro and is home to diverse wildlife, including over 270 species of birds.

When it comes to the climate, Albania experiences a Mediterranean climate along its coastline and a more continental climate in the interior regions. The coastal areas enjoy hot, dry summers and mild, wet winters. The average temperature in the summer months (June to August) ranges from 25°C to 30°C (77°F to 86°F), making it an ideal destination for sun-seekers. The coastal region also benefits from the refreshing sea breezes that provide relief from the heat.

Inland, the climate becomes more continental, with colder winters and hotter summers. The central and northern mountainous regions experience heavy snowfall during the winter months, attracting winter sports enthusiasts. The capital city, Tirana, situated in the western part of the country, experiences a mild climate with average temperatures ranging from 6°C to 14°C (43°F to 57°F) in winter and 21°C to 30°C (70°F to 86°F) in summer.

Due to its diverse topography, Albania's climate varies from region to region. The eastern highlands and the southwestern part of the country are drier and receive less rainfall compared to the western coastal areas. The mountainous areas in the north experience a more alpine climate, with cooler temperatures and higher precipitation.

Albania's geography and climate contribute to its rich biodiversity. The country is home to various plant and animal species, including brown bears, wolves, lynx, and golden eagles. The vast forests that cover a significant portion of the country provide a habitat for diverse flora and fauna.

Albanian Cuisine

Albanian cuisine is a delightful blend of flavors, colors, and traditions that reflect the rich history and diverse cultural influences of the Balkan region. Known for its simplicity, freshness, and use of locally sourced ingredients, Albanian cuisine offers a unique culinary experience that is sure to tantalize the taste buds of any food enthusiast.

History and Influences:

Albanian cuisine has deep historical roots that can be traced back to the Illyrians, an ancient people who inhabited the region thousands of years ago. Over the centuries, Albania has been influenced by neighboring countries such as Greece, Italy, Turkey, and the Balkan states, resulting in a culinary melting pot that combines elements from various cultures.

Key Ingredients:

Albanian cuisine relies heavily on fresh, seasonal ingredients that are readily available in the region. Staple ingredients include vegetables like tomatoes, peppers, eggplants, and cucumbers, as well as legumes such as beans and lentils. Meat, particularly lamb, beef, and poultry, is also commonly used, along with dairy products like cheese and yogurt. Olive oil, garlic, onions, and various herbs and spices, including oregano, basil, and mint, are integral to the flavors of Albanian dishes.

Traditional Dishes:

Byrek: Byrek is a savory pastry filled with ingredients such as cheese, spinach, or meat. It is a popular snack or breakfast item and can be found in different variations across the country.

Tavë Kosi: Tavë Kosi is a traditional Albanian dish consisting of baked lamb or beef with yogurt and eggs. The combination of tender meat, tangy yogurt, and aromatic spices creates a delectable flavor.

Fërgesë: Fërgesë is a hearty dish made with diced meat, peppers, tomatoes, and a variety of cheeses. It is typically served hot and pairs well with traditional Albanian bread.

Qofte: Qofte, or Albanian meatballs, are seasoned ground meat patties that are either grilled or fried. They are often enjoyed with a side of fresh salad or as part of a platter with other mezze-style dishes.

Baklava: Baklava, a sweet pastry made of layers of filo dough filled with nuts and sweetened with honey or syrup, is a popular dessert in Albanian cuisine. It is rich, indulgent, and a perfect ending to a delicious meal.

Eating Customs and Traditions:

Albanians take great pride in their hospitality and love for food. Sharing a meal is an essential part of the Albanian culture, and guests are always welcomed with open arms. It is common to see large, multi-course meals prepared for special occasions and gatherings.

Language and Communication

Language and communication are essential aspects of any society, playing a crucial role in preserving cultural heritage and fostering social cohesion. In Albania, a small Balkan country nestled in the heart of Southeastern Europe, language and communication hold great significance. With a rich linguistic history and a unique blend of influences, Albania's language and communication patterns offer a fascinating glimpse into its diverse culture and people.

Albanian Language:

The Albanian language, known as Shqip, holds a distinct position in the linguistic world as one of the oldest Indo-European languages still spoken today. It belongs to the group of Balkan languages and has two primary dialects: Gheg, primarily spoken in the northern regions, and Tosk, prevalent in the southern parts of the country. Despite these dialectical variations, a unified standard Albanian has been established, ensuring linguistic cohesion and effective communication throughout the country.

Historical Significance:

The roots of the Albanian language can be traced back to ancient Illyrian times, showcasing a rich and uninterrupted history. However, due to historical influences and political changes, the Albanian language faced challenges, including suppression during the Ottoman Empire's rule and efforts to assimilate under Italian and later communist regimes. Despite these obstacles, the resilience of the Albanian people ensured the survival and preservation of their language, which remains a symbol of national identity today.

Bilingualism and Multilingualism:

Albania's geographical proximity to neighboring countries has contributed to a multilingual environment, with many Albanians being proficient in more than one language. In addition to Albanian, significant communities of speakers of Greek, Macedonian, Serbian, and Montenegrin can be found in various regions of the country. This multicultural and multilingual landscape fosters a dynamic exchange of ideas and cultural intermingling.

Language Policy and Education:

Language policy in Albania is centered around the protection, promotion, and cultivation of the Albanian language. Albanian is the sole official language, ensuring its dominance in administrative, educational, and public spheres. The Albanian education system places great emphasis on language instruction, with schools providing education primarily in Albanian, and a focus on teaching foreign languages, most notably English, as a second language.

Media and Literature:

The media landscape in Albania predominantly utilizes the Albanian language, with television, radio, newspapers, and online platforms delivering news and entertainment to the population. The flourishing literary tradition in Albania has produced numerous renowned writers and poets, contributing to the country's cultural wealth and providing a platform for expressing national identity and historical narratives.

Digital Communication and Social Media:

In recent years, digital communication and social media platforms have become an integral part of daily life in Albania. Social networking sites such as Facebook, Instagram, and Twitter have gained immense popularity, offering Albanians a medium to express themselves, connect with others, and share their cultural experiences with the world. This digital era has created new opportunities for global interaction while preserving and promoting the Albanian language.

CHAPTER 2

PRACTICAL INFORMATION

If you are planning to visit Albania, it is essential to have practical information at your fingertips to ensure a smooth and enjoyable trip. From visa requirements to transportation options, this guide will provide you with all the necessary details to navigate Albania with ease.

Visa Requirements

If you're planning to visit Albania, it's essential to familiarize yourself with the country's visa requirements to ensure a smooth and hassle-free journey. In this guide, we will explore the visa requirements for Albania, providing you with the necessary information to plan your trip.

Visa-Free Entry:

First and foremost, it's important to note that citizens from several countries enjoy visa-free entry to Albania. These countries include the member states of the European Union (EU), the United States, Canada, Australia, New Zealand, Japan, South Korea, and many others. Citizens of these countries can enter Albania without a visa and stay for up to 90 days within a 180-day period.

Schengen Visa Holders:

If you hold a valid Schengen visa, you are also allowed to enter Albania without an additional visa. The Schengen visa must have a minimum validity of 5 days and allow for at least two entries. It's important to note that the visa-free entry for Schengen visa holders applies to tourism, business, and family visits only.

Visa on Arrival:

For citizens of countries that do not enjoy visa-free entry or do not hold a valid Schengen visa, Albania offers the option of obtaining a visa on arrival at Tirana International Airport. The visa on arrival is available for tourism, business, medical treatment, and family visits. However, it's recommended to check the official website of the Ministry of Foreign Affairs of Albania or consult with the nearest Albanian embassy or consulate to confirm the eligibility and requirements for visa on arrival, as they may be subject to change.

Visa Requirements:

To enter Albania, whether through visa-free entry, Schengen visa, or visa on arrival, there are several general requirements that must be met. These requirements include:

Valid Passport: Your passport must be valid for at least three months beyond the intended period of stay in Albania. It's advisable to have at least one blank page in your passport for the entry stamp.

Proof of Accommodation: You may be required to present proof of accommodation, such as hotel reservations or an invitation letter from a host, to demonstrate where you will be staying during your visit.

Proof of Sufficient Funds: It is recommended to carry sufficient funds to cover your stay in Albania. This can be in the form of cash, credit cards, or traveler's checks.

Return/Onward Ticket: You may be asked to provide evidence of a return or onward ticket to your home country or another destination.

Travel Insurance: Although not mandatory,

it's highly advisable to have travel insurance that covers medical expenses and emergencies during your stay in Albania.

It's crucial to note that visa requirements and regulations can change periodically, so it's essential to stay updated with the latest information before your trip. Consulting with the official Albanian authorities or your nearest embassy or consulate is the best way to ensure accurate and current information regarding visa requirements.

Currency and Money Matters

When visiting or doing business in Albania, it is essential to have a good understanding of the currency and money matters in the country. In this guide, we will explore the currency used in Albania, its exchange rates, banking system, and essential tips for handling money in the country.

The official currency of Albania is the Albanian Lek (ALL). The Lek is named after the national hero of Albania, Gjergj Kastrioti Skënderbeu, whose image appears on the country's banknotes. The currency is denoted by the symbol "L" and is divided into 100 qindarka, although qindarka coins are no longer in circulation. Banknotes come in denominations of 200, 500, 1000, 2000, and 5000 Lek.

Exchange rates in Albania can fluctuate, so it is advisable to check the current rates before exchanging your currency. The most common foreign currencies exchanged in Albania are the Euro (EUR), US Dollar (USD), and British Pound (GBP). Exchange bureaus can be found throughout the country, particularly in major cities, airports, and tourist areas. It is important to note that exchanging money on the black market is illegal and not recommended.

Albania has a well-developed banking system, with several local and international banks operating in the country. ATMs are widely available in cities and towns, allowing visitors to withdraw cash using their international debit or credit cards. However, it is advisable to carry some cash with you, especially when traveling to more remote areas where ATMs may be scarce.

Credit and debit cards are generally accepted in hotels, restaurants, and larger establishments. However, it is always a good idea to carry some cash for smaller businesses and in case of any unexpected situations. Inform your bank about your travel plans to ensure that your cards will work in Albania and to avoid any potential issues with your accounts.

When using ATMs or paying with cards, be cautious of potential skimming devices and always cover your PIN while entering it. It is also recommended to keep an eye on your transactions and regularly check your bank statements for any unauthorized activity.

In Albania, tipping is not obligatory but is appreciated for good service. It is customary to leave a small tip at restaurants, usually around 5-10% of the bill. Tipping taxi drivers is not common practice, but rounding up the fare to the nearest Lek is considered polite. Hotel staff, tour guides, and other service providers may also appreciate a small gratuity for exceptional service.

Lastly, it is important to note that counterfeit currency can occasionally be an issue in Albania. To avoid receiving counterfeit notes, it is advisable to examine banknotes carefully before accepting them, paying attention to security features such as watermarks, holograms, and color-shifting ink.

Transportation

Albania offers various means of transportation that cater to both locals and tourists. This guide explores the transportation infrastructure in Albania, highlighting its road networks, railways, air travel, and public transportation systems.

Road Networks:

Albania boasts a well-developed road network that connects major cities, towns, and tourist destinations. The country has made significant investments in upgrading its roads and highways, improving accessibility and travel efficiency. The most notable road in Albania is the A1, connecting the capital city of Tirana to the coastal city of Durrës. The A2 and A3 highways also play a crucial role in connecting Albania with neighboring countries such as Greece, Montenegro, and Kosovo. Additionally, Albania has been working on expanding its road infrastructure, including the construction of new motorways, which has further improved transportation within the country.

Railways:

Albania's railway system may not be as extensive as its road network, but it still offers an alternative mode of transportation. The country has a limited but picturesque rail network that provides scenic journeys through stunning landscapes. The main railway line runs from the capital, Tirana, to the northern city of Shkodër and extends further to the Montenegrin border. Although the railway system is currently undergoing modernization and improvement, it remains a charming way to explore the country's diverse terrain.

Air Travel:

Albania is well-connected by air, with international airports serving as gateways to the country. Tirana International Airport Nënë Tereza is the busiest airport, located just outside the capital city. It offers flights to numerous destinations in Europe, serving as a crucial transportation hub for both business and leisure travelers. Additionally, other airports, such as the ones in Vlora, Saranda, and Gjirokastër, cater to seasonal and regional flights, promoting tourism and accessibility to various regions of Albania.

Public Transportation:

Public transportation in Albania is primarily based on bus networks, which serve both short and long-distance travel. Tirana, being the capital city, has an extensive bus network that efficiently connects various neighborhoods and suburbs. Additionally, minibusses, known as furgons, are a popular mode of transportation, especially for intercity travel. Furgons provide an affordable and convenient means of reaching different destinations within the country. The introduction of e-ticketing systems has improved the efficiency and accessibility of public transportation in Albania.

Getting to Albania

If you're planning a trip to Albania, it's important to know how to get there and make the most of your journey. This guide will guide you through the various transportation options available to reach Albania and provide essential information for a smooth travel experience.

By Air:

The quickest and most convenient way to reach Albania is by air. Tirana International Airport Nënë Tereza (TIA), also known as Rinas Airport, is the main international gateway to the country. Situated just 17 kilometers northwest of Tirana, the capital city, it offers numerous direct flights from major cities across Europe. Airlines such as Air Albania, Alitalia, Turkish Airlines, Lufthansa, and Wizz operate regular flights to and from Tirana. Depending on your location, you may also find connecting flights to other Albanian airports, including Ohrid, Saranda, and Vlora.

By Land:

If you prefer a scenic journey or are traveling from a neighboring country, traveling to Albania by land is a viable option. Albania shares its borders with Montenegro, Kosovo, North Macedonia, and Greece, offering multiple entry points for land travel.

Montenegro: If you're coming from Montenegro, you can take a bus from cities like Podgorica or Ulcinj. The journey takes around 4-5 hours, depending on the route and traffic conditions. Alternatively, you can hire a taxi or rent a car for more flexibility.

Kosovo: From Kosovo, you can reach Albania by bus or taxi. The journey from Pristina to Tirana takes approximately 5-6 hours. Keep in mind that during peak travel seasons, it's advisable to book your tickets in advance.

North Macedonia: Buses operate regularly between Skopje, the capital of North Macedonia, and Tirana. The journey usually takes around 4-5 hours. Private taxis and rental cars are also available for travel between the two countries.

Greece: If you're traveling from Greece, you can cross the border by bus, car, or train. Buses are the most common mode of transportation, with routes connecting major Greek cities like Athens and Thessaloniki to Tirana and other Albanian destinations. The journey duration varies depending on the starting point, but it typically ranges from 4 to

8 hours.

By Sea:

Albania boasts a beautiful coastline along the Adriatic and Ionian Seas, making traveling by sea an enchanting option. Ferries operate between Albania and neighboring countries, providing a unique and picturesque way to reach the country.

Italy: Ferries connect the ports of Durres and Vlora in Albania to several Italian ports, including Bari, Brindisi, and Ancona. The journey duration varies depending on the route and can range from 6 to 10 hours.

Greece: Ferries also operate between Albania and Greece, connecting the ports of Saranda and Vlora to Greek islands such as Corfu and Paxos. These routes offer a scenic and leisurely way to travel, with journey times ranging from 30 minutes to 3 hours.

Once you've arrived in Albania, an extensive network of public transportation, including buses, taxis, and rental cars, is available to explore the country further. It's worth noting that driving in Albania can be challenging, especially in rural areas, so it's recommended to familiarize yourself with local driving regulations and road conditions before opting for a rental car.

Accommodation Options

If you're planning a trip to Albania, one of the first things you'll need to consider is your accommodation options. Fortunately, Albania offers a range of choices to suit every budget and preference, from luxury hotels to budget-friendly hostels and unique guesthouses.

Luxury Hotels:

For those seeking the ultimate in comfort and luxury, Albania boasts a selection of high-end hotels that provide a memorable stay. Many of these hotels are located in popular tourist destinations such as Tirana, the capital city, and the picturesque coastal towns of Saranda and Vlora. These luxury establishments offer spacious and elegantly appointed rooms, world-class amenities, including swimming pools, spa facilities, and gourmet restaurants, ensuring an indulgent experience for their guests. Some notable luxury hotels in Albania include the Sheraton Tirana Hotel, Hotel Dajti, and the Maritim Hotel Plaza Tirana.

Boutique Hotels:

If you prefer a more intimate and unique accommodation experience, Albania's boutique hotels are the perfect choice. These smaller, often family-run establishments offer personalized service and a charming atmosphere. Boutique hotels can be found in various locations, including historic towns, coastal resorts, and mountain retreats. They often feature stylish décor, cozy rooms, and distinctive architecture that reflects the local culture. Some popular boutique hotels in Albania include Hotel 3A, Hotel Kotoni, and the charming Hotel Mangalemi in Berat.

Guesthouses:

For a truly immersive and authentic experience, consider staying in a traditional Albanian guesthouse. These guesthouses, known as "kulla" or "kulla e ngorres," can be found in rural areas and provide a glimpse into the country's rich cultural heritage. These unique accommodations are typically renovated old stone houses that have been converted into comfortable lodgings. Guests can enjoy homemade meals prepared with local ingredients and learn about Albanian traditions from their hosts. Examples of guesthouses in Albania include Bujtina e Bardhe in Theth, Villa Gjeçaj in Shkodra, and Rruga Meso Pukë in Puka.

Hostels:

For budget-conscious travelers or those

seeking a more social atmosphere, hostels are an excellent choice. Albania has a growing number of hostels in major cities and popular tourist destinations, offering affordable accommodation options. These hostels often provide dormitory-style rooms, private rooms, and communal areas where guests can socialize and exchange travel tips. Some hostels also organize activities and tours to help visitors explore the country. Notable hostels in Albania include Trip'n'Hostel in Tirana, Hairy Lemon Hostel in Berat, and Mrizi i Zanave in Shkodra.

Vacation Rentals:

Another popular option for accommodation in Albania is vacation rentals, particularly for families or larger groups. Websites like Airbnb offer a wide range of apartments, villas, and houses for short-term stays in various locations across the country. These vacation rentals provide the comforts of home, such as fully equipped kitchens and living areas, allowing guests to have more flexibility during their stay. They are an ideal choice for those who prefer a self-catering experience and want to explore the local culture at their own pace.

Camping:

For nature lovers and adventure seekers, camping is an exciting option to experience Albania's breathtaking landscapes up close. The country is dotted with campsites that provide basic facilities such as toilets, showers, and sometimes even restaurants or small shops. Camping allows visitors to immerse themselves in Albania's natural beauty, whether it's camping by the stunning Albanian Riviera, the majestic Albanian Alps, or in the heart of the national parks. Some popular campsites in Albania include Campsite Gjipe in Dhërmi, Campsite Rilindja in Theth, and Campsite Lake Shkodra Resort in Shkodra.

When planning your trip to Albania, consider the diverse accommodation options available to ensure a comfortable and memorable stay. Whether you prefer luxury, boutique charm, cultural immersion, social interaction, or a budget-friendly experience, Albania has something to offer every traveler. Embrace the warm Albanian hospitality and embark on an unforgettable journey through this enchanting country.

Health and Safety Tips

While exploring this captivating destination, it's essential to prioritize your health and safety. By following certain guidelines and adopting precautionary measures, you can ensure a pleasant and trouble-free experience in Albania. This guide presents a comprehensive guide to health and safety tips that will help you make the most of your visit while keeping yourself protected.

Vaccinations and Health Check-ups:

Before traveling to Albania, it is advisable to consult with your healthcare provider to ensure that you are up to date on routine vaccinations. Additionally, inquire about specific vaccines recommended for travel to Albania, such as hepatitis A and B, typhoid, and tetanus. Consider scheduling a general health check-up to ensure you are in good physical condition for your trip.

Travel Insurance:

Obtaining travel insurance is crucial to protect yourself against unforeseen circumstances during your stay in Albania. Make sure your policy covers medical expenses, emergency medical evacuation, and repatriation in case of illness or injury. Familiarize yourself with the terms and conditions of your insurance to understand what is covered and how to make a claim if necessary.

Safe Food and Water:

To prevent foodborne illnesses, exercise caution while consuming food and beverages in Albania. Stick to bottled water or use water purification methods such as boiling, filtering, or using water purification tablets. Avoid consuming raw or undercooked meats, seafood, and unpeeled fruits and vegetables, unless they have been thoroughly washed and disinfected.

Sun Protection:

Albania boasts a Mediterranean climate with long hours of sunshine, particularly during the summer months. Protect yourself from harmful ultraviolet (UV) radiation by wearing sunscreen with a high sun protection factor (SPF), a wide-brimmed hat, sunglasses, and lightweight clothing that covers your arms and legs. Seek shade during the hottest hours of the day, generally between 11 a.m. and 4 p.m.

Insect Protection:

While Albania is not known for significant health risks related to insect-borne diseases, it is still advisable to protect yourself from mosquito bites. Use insect repellent containing DEET on exposed skin and clothing, particularly during dusk and dawn when mosquitoes are most active. Consider using bed nets and keeping windows and doors closed or screened to minimize the presence of insects in your accommodation.

Road Safety:

If you plan to explore Albania by road, exercise caution and follow traffic rules diligently. Keep in mind that driving habits and road conditions may differ from what you are accustomed to. Always wear seatbelts, use child safety seats where appropriate, and avoid driving under the influence of alcohol or drugs. Be vigilant while crossing roads, as pedestrian safety measures may vary in different areas.

Emergency Services and Medical Facilities:

Familiarize yourself with the local emergency contact numbers in Albania, including the police, ambulance, and fire services. It is also recommended to identify the nearest medical facilities and hospitals in the areas you plan to visit. Carry a copy of your passport, insurance details, and emergency contact information with you at all times.

CHAPTER 3

EXPLORING THE REGIONS

The Capital City

Tirana, the vibrant capital city of Albania, is a place where history meets modernity, where ancient traditions blend seamlessly with contemporary culture. Located in the heart of the country, Tirana serves as a cultural, economic, and political hub, showcasing the unique spirit and character of Albania. From its rich history to its vibrant atmosphere, Tirana has much to offer to locals and visitors alike.

One of the first things that strike visitors upon arrival in Tirana is the city's colorful and eclectic architecture. The cityscape is a mix of styles, reflecting its complex past. Ottoman,

Italian, and Communist-era buildings coexist, creating a fascinating juxtaposition of different architectural periods. Skanderbeg Square, the city's central square, is a prime example of this fusion, with its grand boulevard, mosaic tiles, and landmarks such as the National Historical Museum and the Et'hem Bey Mosque. As you stroll through the streets of Tirana, you'll encounter a blend of modern glass facades and traditional houses, offering a captivating visual feast.

Tirana's history dates back to ancient times, and the city has witnessed the rise and fall of empires throughout the centuries. Originally founded as a small Ottoman town, Tirana has evolved into a bustling metropolis. The city endured periods of occupation and isolation during the 20th century but has since emerged as a symbol of Albania's resilience and progress. Exploring the city's museums and historical sites provides valuable insights into its complex past. The National Historical Museum, Bunk'Art, and the House of Leaves are just a few of the attractions that offer a glimpse into Tirana's history and the struggles its people have faced.

In recent years, Tirana has undergone a remarkable transformation, embracing modernity and innovation. The city has seen extensive urban development projects that have revitalized public spaces, created parks, and improved infrastructure. The transformation of the Blloku neighborhood is a prime example of this urban revival. Once an exclusive enclave for Communist elites, it is now a bustling area filled with trendy cafes, bars, and restaurants, attracting locals and tourists alike. The vibrant street art scene adds an extra layer of creativity and energy to the city, with colorful murals adorning buildings and walls throughout Tirana.

As the cultural center of Albania, Tirana offers a diverse range of artistic and entertainment experiences. The city boasts numerous theaters, galleries, and music venues where visitors can enjoy a variety of performances, exhibitions, and concerts. The National Theater, Palace of Congresses, and the Opera and Ballet Theater are just a few of the venues that showcase the country's rich artistic heritage. Additionally, Tirana hosts various festivals throughout the year, celebrating music, film, and traditional Albanian customs, providing visitors with an opportunity to immerse themselves in the vibrant cultural scene.

Tirana is also a city of parks and green spaces,

offering respite from the bustling urban environment. The Grand Park, with its tranquil lake and lush surroundings, is a favorite spot for locals and visitors to relax, exercise, or enjoy a picnic. The Rinia Park, located near the city center, is a vibrant gathering place, particularly during the evenings when people come together to socialize and enjoy the lively atmosphere.

Cuisine is an essential part of experiencing any culture, and Tirana does not disappoint in this regard. The city is brimming with restaurants and cafes that offer a diverse range of culinary delights, from traditional Albanian dishes to international cuisine. Exploring the local markets, such as the Pazari i Ri, allows visitors to sample fresh produce, cheese, and other traditional products, providing a sensory experience that showcases the flavors of the region.

Tirana's warm and welcoming atmosphere is undoubtedly influenced by the friendliness and hospitality of its people. Albanians are known for their warmth and generosity, always ready to welcome visitors with open arms and share their rich cultural heritage. Engaging with the locals offers a unique opportunity to learn more about their traditions, stories, and way of life.

Local Experiences

One of the most alluring aspects of visiting Albania is the opportunity to immerse yourself in authentic local experiences. Whether you prefer exploring historical sites, indulging in traditional cuisine, or connecting with the friendly locals, Albania has something to offer everyone. Here are some of the top local experiences that should not be missed:

Explore the Ancient City of Butrint: Located in the southern part of Albania, Butrint is an archaeological site that dates back to the 7th century BC. As you wander through the ruins of this UNESCO World Heritage site, you'll be transported back in time, marveling at the ancient temples, theaters, and fortifications. The serene surroundings, including a beautiful lake and lush forests, make Butrint a truly enchanting place to visit.

Discover the Albanian Riviera: Stretching along the southwestern coastline, the Albanian Riviera is a paradise for beach lovers and nature enthusiasts. Explore the pristine beaches, such as Ksamil and Dhermi, with their crystal-clear turquoise waters and white sandy shores. Hike the Llogara National Park for breathtaking views of the coastline, or venture off the beaten path to discover hidden coves and secluded bays.

Experience Traditional Village Life: To truly understand the soul of Albania, venture into the countryside and visit traditional villages. Places like Theth, Valbona, and Berat offer a glimpse into the country's rich cultural heritage. Stay in traditional guesthouses, taste homemade Albanian cuisine, and engage with locals who are eager to share their traditions and stories.

Sample Albanian Cuisine: Food is an integral part of Albanian culture, and indulging in local cuisine is a must-do experience. Try dishes like Tavë Kosi (baked lamb with yogurt), Fërgesë (a traditional cheese and peppers dish), and Baklava (a sweet pastry). Visit local markets to taste fresh produce and sample traditional cheeses, olive oil, and honey. Don't forget to pair your meal with a glass of local wine or raki, a traditional Albanian brandy.

Attend a Traditional Festival: Albania is known for its vibrant celebrations and festivals, which offer a unique insight into the country's traditions and customs. The National Folk Festival in Gjirokastër and the Kruja Carnival are just a few examples of the lively events that take place throughout the year. Immerse yourself in the music, dance, and colorful costumes, and join the locals in their joyful celebrations.

As you engage in these local experiences, you'll discover the genuine warmth and hospitality of the Albanian people. They are proud of their heritage and eager to share it with visitors, making your journey through Albania a truly unforgettable one.

Dining and Nightlife

Albania boasts a vibrant dining scene and an exciting nightlife that is sure to captivate both locals and tourists alike. From traditional Albanian cuisine to international flavors, and from bustling bars to energetic clubs, Albania offers a diverse range of options for dining and nighttime entertainment.

Albanian cuisine is a delightful fusion of Mediterranean and Balkan flavors, reflecting the country's geographic location and influences from neighboring Greece, Italy, and Turkey. One cannot visit Albania without indulging in the national dish, Tavë Kosi. This mouthwatering baked lamb and yogurt casserole, served with a side of fluffy rice, is a true gastronomic delight. Seafood lovers will be thrilled with the abundance of fresh catch available along the coastline, prepared in various styles such as grilled, fried, or stewed. For those seeking vegetarian options, Albanian cuisine offers delectable dishes like Byrek, a savory pastry filled with spinach, cheese, or meat, and Fërgesë, a hearty blend of peppers, tomatoes, and cottage cheese. To complement these culinary delights, make sure to sample the local wine and rakia, a traditional fruit brandy.

When it comes to nightlife, Albania offers a diverse range of experiences to suit every taste. The capital city, Tirana, is a vibrant hub that comes alive after sunset. Blloku, once an exclusive residential area, has transformed into a trendy district with a plethora of bars, clubs, and lounges. Here, you can sip on handcrafted cocktails, dance to the beats of local and international DJs, and mingle with a stylish crowd. For a more laid-back evening, head to the enchanting coastal city of Saranda. Along its palm-lined promenade, you'll find an array of cozy bars and waterfront restaurants, where you can enjoy breathtaking sunsets while savoring delicious cocktails and fresh seafood. The cities of Durrës and Vlora also offer a vibrant nightlife scene, with beachside clubs and live music venues that keep the party going until the early hours of the morning.

Beyond the urban centers, Albania's charming towns and picturesque villages provide unique dining experiences. In the UNESCO World Heritage Site of Berat, known as the "City of a Thousand Windows," you can dine in traditional Ottoman-style houses converted into restaurants. Enjoy a leisurely meal while surrounded by ancient architecture and panoramic views of the city's fortress. The town of Gjirokastër, another UNESCO World Heritage Site, offers a similar experience, with cozy taverns serving local delicacies amidst a medieval ambiance.

It is worth noting that Albanian hospitality plays a significant role in enhancing the dining and nightlife experiences. The warmth and friendliness of the locals create an inviting atmosphere, making visitors feel like part of the community. Whether you're dining at a family-run restaurant or enjoying a night out in a bustling club, you're likely to be greeted with genuine smiles and warm welcomes.

Northern Albania

Northern Albania is a captivating region that offers a wealth of natural beauty, cultural heritage, and adventurous opportunities. This hidden gem is a paradise for nature enthusiasts, history buffs, and those seeking an off-the-beaten-path experience.

One of the most prominent features of Northern Albania is its breathtaking landscapes. The Albanian Alps, also known as the Accursed Mountains, dominate the skyline with their rugged peaks and deep valleys. This untamed wilderness is a hiker's paradise, offering countless trails that lead to hidden waterfalls, pristine lakes, and remote villages. The Valbona Valley, Theth National Park, and the Karaburun-Sazan Marine Park are just a few of the many natural wonders waiting to be explored.

In addition to its natural beauty, Northern Albania is steeped in history and rich cultural heritage. The region is home to ancient castles, Ottoman-era towns, and vibrant traditional communities. The city of Shkodra, located on the shores of Lake Shkodra, is a cultural hub with its historic castle, bustling bazaar, and renowned museums. The Rozafa Castle, perched high on a hill overlooking the city, offers panoramic views and a fascinating glimpse into the region's past.

For those seeking a taste of authentic Albanian culture, a visit to the traditional villages of Theth and Valbona is a must. These remote mountain settlements have preserved their centuries-old customs and offer a unique glimpse into traditional Albanian life. Here, visitors can stay in guesthouses run by local families, savor homemade Albanian cuisine, and participate in traditional activities such as folk dancing and handicraft workshops.

Northern Albania is also blessed with a diverse array of flora and fauna. The region is home to rare and endangered species, making it a haven for nature lovers and wildlife enthusiasts. The Balkan Lynx, the Dalmatian Pelican, and the Balkan chamois are just a few of the remarkable species that call this region home. Exploring the forests, wetlands, and protected areas of Northern Albania is a chance to witness the incredible biodiversity of the area and contribute to its conservation.

In recent years, adventure tourism has gained popularity in Northern Albania. The region offers a wide range of activities, including hiking, mountain biking, kayaking, and paragliding. The rugged terrain and untamed rivers provide adrenaline-pumping experiences for thrill-seekers, while the pristine landscapes offer a serene backdrop for those seeking a peaceful retreat. The Via Dinarica, an internationally recognized hiking trail, passes through Northern Albania, attracting outdoor enthusiasts from around the world.

To fully experience the wonders of Northern Albania, it is essential to immerse oneself in the warmth and hospitality of the locals. The people of this region are known for their friendliness and welcoming nature. Visitors have the opportunity to engage with the locals, learn about their traditions, and share memorable experiences. Homestays and village tourism initiatives allow travelers to forge genuine connections and gain a deeper understanding of Albanian culture and way of life.

Central Albania

Central Albania is a region that captivates visitors with its rich history, natural beauty, and warm hospitality. Steeped in tradition and offering a diverse array of experiences, this enchanting part of the country is a must-visit destination for those seeking to explore the true essence of Albania.

Historical Heritage:

Central Albania is a treasure trove of historical sites, showcasing the region's deep-rooted past. The city of Kruja is a notable highlight, renowned for its majestic castle perched on a hilltop. This fortress, once the stronghold of national hero Skanderbeg, offers panoramic views of the surrounding landscape and houses a fascinating museum dedicated to Albania's struggle for independence.

Another iconic destination is the ancient city of Apollonia, founded in the 6th century BCE. Explore its well-preserved ruins, including a magnificent amphitheater, ancient temples, and an impressive library. The nearby town of Berat, known as the "City of a Thousand Windows," boasts a UNESCO World Heritage-listed old town with Ottoman-era architecture and stunning Byzantine churches.

Natural Wonders:

Central Albania's landscape is a playground for nature enthusiasts. The region is home to the breathtaking Dajti Mountain National Park, just a short drive from the bustling capital city, Tirana. Hop on the cable car and ascend to the summit for stunning views of Tirana and the surrounding countryside.

Lake Ohrid, shared with North Macedonia, offers tranquil beauty and is a UNESCO World Heritage site. Explore the charming town of Pogradec on the lake's shores, stroll along the promenade, and savor the local cuisine while taking in the picturesque views.

Central Albania is also blessed with a wealth of national parks and protected areas, including the Shebenik-Jabllanice National Park and the Divjaka-Karavasta National Park. Hike through lush forests, spot rare bird species, or relax on pristine sandy beaches, all within easy reach.

Cultural Experiences:

Immerse yourself in Albanian culture through the region's vibrant festivals, traditional music, and warm hospitality. Witness the lively celebrations during the Tirana International Film Festival, showcasing the best of Albanian and international cinema. Experience the rich folklore traditions in Elbasan during the annual "Dita e Verës" (Summer Day) festival, where locals don colorful traditional costumes and participate in vibrant street parades.

Food lovers will delight in Central Albania's culinary offerings. Indulge in delicious local dishes such as byrek (savory pie), tavë kosi (baked lamb with yogurt), and qofte (meatballs). Sample the renowned Albanian raki or wine produced from the region's vineyards.

Warm Hospitality:

The people of Central Albania are known for their warm and welcoming nature. Whether you're exploring the cobblestone streets of Berat or venturing into the remote mountain villages, you'll be greeted with genuine hospitality and a genuine curiosity about your journey. Engage with the locals, learn about their customs, and gain insights into their way of life.

Southern Albania

Southern Albania offers a unique and unforgettable experience. Join us on a journey through this enchanting part of the country, where ancient traditions meet stunning landscapes.

A Tapestry of Natural Splendor:

Southern Albania is blessed with an array of breathtaking landscapes that will leave nature enthusiasts in awe. The Albanian Riviera, stretching along the Ionian coast, presents a stunning combination of turquoise waters, hidden coves, and rugged cliffs. Picture-perfect beaches such as Ksamil and Himara invite visitors to unwind in their pristine surroundings. Venture inland, and you'll encounter the majestic Llogara National Park, where dense forests, alpine meadows, and panoramic views await. Hiking enthusiasts can tackle the mighty Mount Cika for an unforgettable adventure.

Timeless History and Cultural Heritage:

Southern Albania's historical legacy is evident in its numerous archaeological sites and ancient ruins. Explore the UNESCO World Heritage Site of Butrint, an ancient city that dates back to the 8th century BC. Wander through its well-preserved amphitheater, temples, and fortifications, and imagine the stories of past civilizations. Gjirokastër, a UNESCO-listed city, is another highlight, renowned for its Ottoman-era architecture and the magnificent Gjirokastër Castle. The city's cobblestone streets and traditional stone houses provide a glimpse into Albania's rich cultural heritage.

Coastal Charms and Vibrant Towns:

The coastal towns of Saranda and Vlora are vibrant hubs that offer a unique blend of history, culture, and seaside charm. Saranda, known as the "Pearl of the South," beckons visitors with its promenade lined with cafes, restaurants, and lively nightlife. Don't miss the chance to explore the ancient synagogue and the mesmerizing Blue Eye Spring nearby. Vlora, with its scenic waterfront and elegant boulevards, is a gateway to the Albanian Riviera and a popular spot for sailing enthusiasts.

Gastronomy and Culinary Delights:

Southern Albania's cuisine is a delightful fusion of Mediterranean and Balkan flavors. Indulge in traditional dishes such as "byrek" (a savory pastry filled with cheese or spinach), "tavë kosi" (baked lamb with yogurt), and fresh seafood delicacies. The region's fertile lands yield an abundance of olives, citrus fruits, and aromatic herbs, contributing to the richness of its culinary offerings. Savor local wines and raki, an Albanian spirit, to complete your gastronomic journey.

Warm Hospitality and Authentic Experiences:

One of the greatest treasures of Southern Albania is its warm and welcoming people. Discover the true essence of Albanian culture by engaging with locals, visiting traditional villages, and participating in traditional festivals. Experience the warmth of Albanian hospitality firsthand as you immerse yourself in the customs, music, and folklore of this fascinating region. Local guides and guesthouses offer authentic experiences, providing insights into the unique way of life in Southern Albania.

Coastal Riviera

Albania's Coastal Riviera is a hidden gem in the heart of the Balkans. With its untouched natural beauty, charming seaside towns, and warm Mediterranean climate, this coastal paradise offers an unforgettable vacation experience. From stunning beaches to rich cultural heritage, Albania's Riviera has something for everyone, whether you're seeking relaxation, adventure, or a taste of traditional Albanian hospitality.

Beaches:

Albania's Coastal Riviera is renowned for its breathtaking beaches that rival those of more famous Mediterranean destinations. From sandy stretches to secluded coves, the coastline offers a diverse range of coastal landscapes. Ksamil Beach, with its crystal-clear turquoise waters and powdery white sand, is often compared to the stunning beaches of the Caribbean. Dhërmi Beach, tucked away between rugged cliffs, offers a tranquil setting with azure waters, making it perfect for sunbathing and swimming. Furthermore, Jale Beach, Himara Beach, and Gjipe Beach are among the other pristine coastal gems that visitors can explore along the Riviera.

Picturesque Towns:

The Coastal Riviera is dotted with picturesque towns and villages, each with its own unique character and charm. Saranda, a bustling coastal town, serves as the gateway to the Riviera and offers a vibrant atmosphere with its waterfront promenade, lively cafes, and a rich history that includes remnants of ancient civilizations. The town of Himara, perched on a hillside overlooking the sea, exudes a laid-back vibe and rewards visitors with breathtaking views. The colorful houses of Vlorë and the historic streets of Berat add to the Riviera's allure, providing a glimpse into Albania's cultural heritage.

Outdoor Activities:

For adventure seekers, the Coastal Riviera is a playground of outdoor activities. Hiking enthusiasts can explore the Llogara National Park, a mountainous paradise that offers breathtaking views of the Adriatic Sea and the surrounding landscapes. The park is home to diverse flora and fauna, making it a haven for nature lovers. Water sports enthusiasts can indulge in snorkeling, scuba diving, and kayaking, discovering the rich marine life and hidden caves along the coast. Additionally, the Riviera's favorable winds make it an ideal destination for windsurfing and kitesurfing.

Culinary Delights:

Albania's Coastal Riviera is a paradise for food lovers. The region boasts a unique culinary tradition that blends Mediterranean flavors with distinct Albanian influences. Visitors can savor delicious seafood dishes, such as fresh grilled fish and octopus, served with locally sourced ingredients and traditional recipes. Alongside seafood, the Riviera offers a variety of mouthwatering dishes, including savory pies, lamb dishes, and a wide range of dairy products. Don't forget to pair your meals with a glass of local wine or rakia, Albania's traditional fruit brandy.

Cultural Heritage:

The Coastal Riviera is steeped in history and culture, providing visitors with a glimpse into

Albania's rich heritage. The ancient city of Butrint, a UNESCO World Heritage Site, is a must-visit destination. This archaeological marvel showcases the remains of a once-flourishing Greek and Roman city, including a theater, temples, and fortifications. Gjirokastër, another UNESCO World Heritage Site, is a beautifully preserved Ottoman-era town known for its stone houses and cobbled streets. Exploring these historical sites allows travelers to immerse themselves in Albania's fascinating past.

Off-the-Beaten-Path Destinations

While popular tourist destinations like Tirana and the Albanian Riviera receive a fair share of attention, there are numerous off-the-beaten-path destinations that remain largely undiscovered by the masses. In this guide, we will delve into some of these hidden treasures, providing you with a glimpse of the lesser-known wonders that Albania has to offer.

Gjirokastër:

Located in southern Albania, Gjirokastër is a UNESCO World Heritage Site renowned for its well-preserved Ottoman architecture and captivating medieval charm. Stroll through its cobblestone streets and marvel at the ancient stone houses that line the hillside. Explore the imposing Gjirokastër Fortress, which offers panoramic views of the city and houses an intriguing military museum. Immerse yourself in the town's history as you visit the Ethnographic Museum, which provides a glimpse into traditional Albanian life.

Valbona Valley:

Escape to the rugged beauty of the Valbona Valley in northern Albania. This remote and picturesque region offers breathtaking landscapes, including towering peaks, crystal-clear rivers, and dense forests. Embark on a trek along the Valbona River, passing through quaint villages and witnessing traditional rural life. Experience the warmth of Albanian hospitality by staying in one of the guesthouses dotting the valley, where you can savor delicious homemade food and immerse yourself in the local culture.

Berat:

Often referred to as the "City of a Thousand Windows," Berat is another UNESCO World Heritage Site that captivates visitors with its stunning architecture and rich history. The highlight of Berat is its well-preserved medieval fortress, which overlooks the city. Explore the narrow alleys of the old town, where white Ottoman houses are nestled side by side. Don't miss a visit to the Onufri Museum, which houses a remarkable collection of religious icons painted by the renowned Albanian master Onufri.

Butrint:

Step back in time at the ancient city of Butrint, located in the southwestern part of Albania. This archaeological site showcases the remains of civilizations dating back to the

Greeks, Romans, Byzantines, and Venetians. Wander through the ancient ruins, including a well-preserved theater, a Roman forum, and a Venetian castle. Discover the secrets of this UNESCO World Heritage Site, surrounded by a lush national park and the sparkling waters of Lake Butrint.

Theth:

For nature enthusiasts seeking an authentic mountain experience, Theth is a must-visit destination. Nestled in the Albanian Alps, this remote village offers breathtaking vistas, crystal-clear rivers, and pristine landscapes. Explore the Grunas Waterfall and embark on challenging hikes to the Valbona Pass or the Blue Eye, a natural spring that forms a mesmerizing turquoise pool. Experience the unique tradition of the "kanun," a set of ancient Albanian laws, and savor local

delicacies in traditional guesthouses.

CHAPTER 4

OUTDOOR ADVENTURES

Hiking and Trekking

Albania offers a hidden gem for outdoor enthusiasts and nature lovers alike. With its rugged mountains, pristine lakes, and picturesque landscapes, this lesser-explored destination is a paradise for hiking and trekking enthusiasts. From challenging trails that test your endurance to peaceful walks that allow you to soak in the tranquility of nature, Albania's diverse terrain caters to all levels of adventurers. Embark on a journey of discovery as we delve into the captivating world of hiking and trekking in Albania.

Unspoiled Wilderness:

Albania boasts an extraordinary diversity of

landscapes, ranging from towering peaks to deep canyons and verdant valleys. The Albanian Alps, also known as the Accursed Mountains, present a captivating challenge for seasoned hikers. As you ascend through lush alpine meadows, you'll be rewarded with breathtaking panoramas of jagged peaks, glistening glaciers, and crystal-clear lakes. Peaks such as Mount Korab, the highest in the country, offer an exhilarating experience for those seeking to conquer new heights.

Theth National Park:

One of the crown jewels of Albanian hiking destinations is Theth National Park. Tucked away in the northern part of the country, this pristine wilderness boasts a wealth of natural wonders. Trek through narrow paths that lead to the iconic "Blue Eye," a mesmerizing turquoise waterfall nestled amidst limestone cliffs. Immerse yourself in the local culture as you explore traditional stone houses and encounter warm hospitality in the mountain villages.

Valbona Valley:

Adjacent to Theth National Park lies the breathtaking Valbona Valley, a haven for trekkers seeking untouched beauty. Traverse through ancient forests, cross suspension bridges, and witness the powerful force of the Valbona River cascading through the valley. The renowned Peaks of the Balkans trail, connecting Albania with Montenegro and Kosovo, weaves through this enchanting landscape, offering a truly transnational adventure.

Llogara National Park and the Albanian Riviera:

For hikers longing for a coastal escape, the Llogara National Park and the Albanian Riviera provide a unique blend of rugged mountains and azure waters. The Llogara Pass offers mesmerizing vistas of the Ionian Sea, while hiking trails lead to hidden beaches and secluded coves waiting to be explored. The coastal town of Saranda acts as an excellent base for adventures, with nearby attractions like the ancient ruins of Butrint and the UNESCO-listed Gjirokastër offering cultural delights.

Logistics and Safety:

Albania's emerging reputation as a hiking and trekking destination is matched by the country's efforts to improve infrastructure and support outdoor enthusiasts. A growing number of local tour operators offer guided hikes, ensuring safety and providing valuable insights into the region's natural and cultural heritage. It's essential to come prepared with suitable equipment, sturdy footwear, and sufficient supplies, as some trails can be challenging and remote.

Beaches and Water Sports

Albania is a hidden gem for beach lovers and adventure seekers. From sunbathing and swimming to thrilling water sports, this Mediterranean paradise offers a plethora of experiences for all.

Albania's coastline stretches over 450 kilometers, providing ample opportunities for beach enthusiasts to soak up the sun and enjoy the refreshing sea breeze. The country is home to a diverse range of beaches, from secluded coves to bustling resorts. One of the most renowned beach destinations in Albania is the Albanian Riviera, located in the southwestern part of the country. With its white sandy beaches, azure waters, and breathtaking landscapes, the Albanian Riviera is a haven for beach lovers.

One of the most popular beach towns along the Albanian Riviera is Saranda. This vibrant coastal city boasts a vibrant atmosphere and a stunning waterfront promenade lined with cafes, restaurants, and bars. Visitors can relax on Saranda's pristine beaches, take a dip in the crystal-clear waters, or explore nearby attractions such as the ancient archaeological site of Butrint. Saranda also serves as a gateway to the famous Ksamil Islands, a small archipelago with turquoise waters and sandy beaches that are perfect for snorkeling and swimming.

For those seeking a more secluded beach experience, the Albanian Riviera offers hidden gems such as Dhermi and Himara. Dhermi is renowned for its untouched natural beauty, with its long sandy beach framed by towering cliffs. Himara, on the other hand, offers a more tranquil setting with its picturesque bay and pristine pebble beaches. These hidden coastal towns provide a peaceful escape for visitors looking to unwind and enjoy the serenity of the Albanian coastline.

In addition to its stunning beaches, Albania is a paradise for water sports enthusiasts. With its favorable wind conditions and calm seas, the country offers a wide range of thrilling water sports activities. Kitesurfing and windsurfing are particularly popular along the Albanian Riviera, attracting both beginners and experienced riders. The beaches of Karaburun Peninsula and Vlora are known for their excellent wind conditions, making them ideal spots for adrenaline-filled adventures on the water.

Scuba diving and snorkeling are also popular activities in Albania, allowing visitors to explore the rich marine life beneath the surface. The Albanian coastline is home to several underwater caves, reefs, and shipwrecks, providing an exciting playground for divers. The waters of Saranda and Vlora are especially known for their underwater treasures, offering divers a chance to discover colorful coral reefs, schools of fish, and even ancient artifacts.

For those who prefer a more relaxed water sports experience, Albania's coastal towns offer opportunities for kayaking, paddleboarding, and jet skiing. Exploring the picturesque bays and hidden coves by kayak or paddleboard allows visitors to appreciate the natural beauty of the Albanian coastline at their own pace. Jet skiing offers an exhilarating way to navigate the sparkling waters and enjoy the thrill of speed.

Mountain Biking

Whether you are an experienced mountain biker or a novice looking to explore this exciting sport, Albania has something to offer everyone.

One of the most captivating aspects of mountain biking in Albania is the country's rich natural beauty. From the majestic peaks of the Accursed Mountains in the north to the stunning coastline along the Adriatic and Ionian Seas, there is no shortage of breathtaking vistas to discover. The country's diverse terrain caters to a variety of riding styles, from adrenaline-pumping downhill descents to epic cross-country trails.

One popular destination for mountain biking in Albania is Theth National Park, located in the Albanian Alps. Here, riders can tackle challenging trails while being surrounded by awe-inspiring scenery, including cascading waterfalls, dense forests, and snow-capped peaks. The park offers a range of trails suitable for different skill levels, making it an ideal choice for both beginners and advanced riders.

For those seeking a coastal adventure, the Albanian Riviera is a must-visit. The region boasts a network of trails that wind through olive groves, quaint villages, and pristine beaches. The combination of breathtaking sea views and exhilarating biking trails creates an unforgettable experience for riders of all levels. The coastal town of Vlora, with its vibrant atmosphere and proximity to the Llogara National Park, is an excellent starting point for exploring the Albanian Riviera on two wheels.

Another hidden gem for mountain biking enthusiasts is the Valbona Valley National Park. Situated in the northern part of the country, this remote and untouched wilderness offers an incredible range of trails that lead through ancient forests, wildflower meadows, and crystal-clear rivers. The park's rugged terrain and stunning landscapes provide a true backcountry experience, making it a favorite among adventure-seeking mountain bikers.

Albania's emerging mountain biking scene is supported by a growing number of local guides and tour operators who are passionate about sharing their country's natural wonders with visitors. These experts provide valuable insights into the best trails, offer equipment rentals, and organize guided tours tailored to various skill levels and interests. Their knowledge and expertise ensure that riders have a safe and enjoyable experience while exploring the country's biking trails.

Apart from its captivating landscapes, mountain biking in Albania also offers an opportunity to immerse oneself in the country's rich cultural heritage. Exploring remote villages along the biking routes allows riders to interact with friendly locals, sample traditional Albanian cuisine, and gain a deeper understanding of the country's history and traditions.

When planning a mountain biking trip to Albania, it is important to consider the best time to visit. The spring and autumn months, from April to June and September to November, offer pleasant temperatures and less crowded trails. The summer months can be quite hot, especially in the coastal regions, while the winter brings snow and limited biking opportunities in the higher mountain areas.

Rafting and Kayaking

Whether you are a seasoned adventurer or a novice looking for a thrilling experience, Albania's rivers provide an unforgettable journey filled with excitement, challenge, and natural beauty.

A Paradise for Rafting and Kayaking:

Albania boasts an extensive network of rivers, making it a paradise for rafting and kayaking enthusiasts. The country is blessed with several prominent rivers, including the Vjosa, Osum, Devoll, and Shkumbin, each offering unique experiences and challenges for water sports enthusiasts. These rivers wind their way through stunning canyons, remote valleys, and untouched landscapes, providing an unforgettable backdrop for thrilling adventures.

The Vjosa River: A Jewel of Albanian Rafting:

Among Albania's many rivers, the Vjosa stands out as a crown jewel for rafting enthusiasts. Known as the last wild river in Europe, the Vjosa meanders through untouched landscapes, offering an unparalleled rafting experience. The river's crystal-clear turquoise waters, picturesque canyons, and vibrant biodiversity create a perfect setting for an exhilarating journey. Whether you're an adrenaline junkie seeking Class III and IV rapids or a leisurely paddler enjoying the scenic beauty, the Vjosa River has something to offer for everyone.

Exploring the Osum River: Kayaking through Nature's Masterpiece:

For kayaking enthusiasts, the Osum River presents an incredible opportunity to immerse yourself in Albania's natural wonders. Flowing through the Osumi Canyon, one of Europe's most stunning river canyons, the Osum River offers a unique kayaking experience. As you navigate the river's emerald-green waters, you'll encounter awe-inspiring waterfalls, towering cliffs, and lush vegetation, creating a truly enchanting atmosphere. Whether you're a beginner or an experienced kayaker, the Osum River promises an adventure that combines excitement with serene natural beauty.

Adventure for All Levels:

Albania's rivers cater to individuals of all skill levels, from beginners seeking a gentle introduction to water sports to experienced thrill-seekers looking for challenging rapids. Rafting and kayaking tours in Albania are led by experienced guides who provide expert instruction and ensure the safety of participants. Whether you're embarking on a family-friendly rafting trip or an adrenaline-pumping kayaking expedition, the country's adventure tourism infrastructure ensures a memorable experience for everyone.

Cultural and Natural Delights Beyond the Waters:

While the thrill of rafting and kayaking in Albania is an experience in itself, the country offers much more to explore. Rich in history and culture, Albania boasts ancient cities, archaeological sites, and charming traditional villages that are worth exploring before or after your water adventure. You can discover the UNESCO World Heritage Sites of Berat and Gjirokastër, marvel at the stunning Albanian Riviera, or hike in the breathtaking Albanian Alps. Immerse yourself in the warm hospitality of the locals, savor delicious traditional cuisine, and learn about the country's vibrant traditions and customs.

Caving

There is an underground world waiting to be discovered—the captivating realm of Albanian caves. Caving, also known as spelunking, has gained popularity among adventure enthusiasts, providing a unique opportunity to delve into the depths of Albania's subterranean wonders. Let us embark on a thrilling journey to explore the mesmerizing caving experiences that Albania has to offer.

Albania boasts an impressive array of caves, each with its own distinctive allure. From massive underground chambers to intricate cave systems, the country's caves offer a wealth of geological formations, fascinating histories, and incredible biodiversity. One of the most renowned cave systems is the famous "Pellumbas Cave," located near the capital city of Tirana. This cave, with its remarkable stalactites and stalagmites, has become a popular destination for both novice and experienced cavers.

Venturing into the depths of Albanian caves is an awe-inspiring experience that takes visitors on a journey through time. These geological wonders have been formed over millions of years, shaped by the relentless forces of nature. Some caves, such as the "Shpella e Tëllurit" (Cave of Wonders) in Bulqiza, offer a glimpse into the ancient history of the Earth, with their unique mineral formations and underground rivers.

The exploration of Albanian caves is not limited to their geological marvels; it also offers an opportunity to unearth cultural treasures. Many caves served as shelters and hiding places during different periods of Albania's history. These hidden chambers bear witness to the country's past struggles and resilience. The "Pirrogoshi Cave," for instance, played a significant role during World War II as a hideout for the Albanian resistance fighters. Exploring these historic caves provides a deeper understanding of Albania's rich heritage.

Caving in Albania is not solely reserved for the experienced spelunkers. The country offers a range of caves suitable for all levels of expertise, from beginners to seasoned adventurers. Professional guides are available to lead expeditions, ensuring safety and providing valuable insights into the caves' geological and historical significance. They equip participants with the necessary gear, including helmets and headlamps, ensuring an unforgettable and secure caving experience.

One cannot underestimate the importance of responsible caving practices. The delicate ecosystems within caves require preservation and conservation. Visitors are encouraged to follow ethical guidelines, respecting the fragile underground habitats and refraining from disturbing the natural formations. By promoting sustainable caving tourism, Albania aims to preserve these wonders for future generations and raise awareness about the importance of environmental stewardship.

The allure of Albanian caves extends beyond their natural beauty. The adrenaline rush and sense of exploration that accompany caving create a unique bond between individuals and the subterranean world. Whether it's squeezing through narrow passages, rappelling down vertical drops, or wading through underground rivers, the challenges and rewards of caving in Albania are unparalleled.

As you emerge from the depths, covered in the dust of ancient earth, you'll carry with you memories and experiences that will last a lifetime. Caving in Albania is an unforgettable adventure, a chance to step out of your comfort zone and discover a hidden world beneath the surface. So, gear up, embrace the thrill, and let Albania's caves unveil their captivating secrets to you.

CHAPTER 5

CULTURAL EXPERIENCES

Traditional Festivals and Events

One of the best ways to immerse oneself in Albanian culture is by experiencing the traditional festivals and events celebrated throughout the year. From ancient pagan rituals to religious celebrations, these vibrant gatherings showcase the unique customs, folklore, and hospitality that define the Albanian spirit. This guide will explore some of the most captivating traditional festivals and events in Albania, offering a glimpse into the country's cultural tapestry.

Kënga e Tushës (The Tush Song Festival):

Taking place in the picturesque Tushemisht village near Lake Ohrid, Kënga e Tushës is an annual folk music festival held in late August. This event celebrates the traditional songs and dances of the Tush people, an ethnic group residing in the region. The festival brings together renowned folk musicians and singers, captivating audiences with soulful melodies and vibrant performances. Visitors can also indulge in local delicacies, witness traditional handicrafts, and experience the warm hospitality of the Tush community.

Korce Carnival:

The Korce Carnival, held in the city of Korce during late winter or early spring, is a lively event that dates back to the early 20th century. This carnival is a riotous celebration of Albanian folklore and tradition, featuring colorful parades, extravagant costumes, and vibrant masquerades. Participants, both locals and visitors, take to the streets, dancing and singing to the beat of traditional music. The Korce Carnival showcases the exuberance and creativity of the Albanian people, providing a joyous atmosphere for all.

Dita e Verës (Summer Day):

Dita e Verës, also known as Summer Day, is a pagan festival celebrated on March 14th each year. It marks the arrival of spring and the awakening of nature after the long winter months. The festivities include bonfires, traditional dances, and folk performances, with people wearing vibrant clothing and adorning themselves with flowers. Dita e Verës is a time for Albanians to reconnect with their agrarian roots, celebrate fertility, and embrace the beauty of the changing seasons.

Tirana International Film Festival (TIFF):

While not exclusively a traditional festival, the Tirana International Film Festival deserves a mention for its cultural significance. Held annually in the capital city of Tirana, TIFF showcases the best of Albanian and international cinema. The festival provides a platform for filmmakers to exhibit their work, fostering cultural exchange and promoting the art of filmmaking in Albania. It also features workshops, seminars, and retrospectives, making it an enriching experience for both film enthusiasts and industry professionals.

Gjirokastër National Folklore Festival:

Gjirokastër, a UNESCO World Heritage Site renowned for its well-preserved Ottoman-era architecture, hosts the National Folklore Festival every five years. This grand event brings together folklore groups, dancers, musicians, and artists from all regions of Albania, as well as neighboring countries. The festival showcases traditional music, dance performances, and craft exhibitions, creating an enchanting atmosphere that highlights the country's diverse cultural heritage.

UNESCO World Heritage Sites

Albania's World Heritage Sites offer visitors a captivating journey through time. In this book, we will explore some of the remarkable UNESCO World Heritage Sites in Albania.

Historic Centres of Berat and Gjirokastër:

The historic centers of Berat and Gjirokastër are two remarkable towns that have preserved their Ottoman-era architecture. The city of Berat, known as the "City of a Thousand Windows," boasts well-preserved medieval structures, including the iconic Berat Castle, which offers panoramic views of the town. Gjirokastër, on the other hand, is famous for its stone houses, narrow streets, and the imposing Gjirokastër Castle. Both cities provide visitors with an immersive experience in Albania's rich history and culture.

Butrint:

Located in the south of Albania, Butrint is an exceptional archaeological site that dates back to ancient times. This well-preserved ancient city showcases the remnants of various civilizations, including the Greeks, Romans, Byzantines, and Venetians. Visitors can explore the remains of a theater, a basilica, a Roman forum, and other fascinating structures. Surrounded by a beautiful natural landscape, Butrint is not only a cultural treasure but also a picturesque destination.

Natural and Cultural Heritage of the Ohrid Region:

Straddling the border between Albania and North Macedonia, the Ohrid Region is renowned for its natural and cultural significance. Lake Ohrid, one of Europe's oldest and deepest lakes, is the centerpiece of the region. It is home to numerous endemic species and offers breathtaking scenery. The region also includes the town of Ohrid, which features an enchanting Old Town with medieval churches, monasteries, and the iconic Samuel's Fortress. This UNESCO site showcases the harmonious coexistence of nature and cultural heritage.

Ancient City of Butrint:

Situated on a hill overlooking the Vjosa River, the ancient city of Butrint is a testament to Albania's rich history. Founded by the Greeks in the 7th century BC, Butrint thrived under Roman rule and later became a Byzantine stronghold. Today, visitors can explore the ruins of a theater, Roman baths, an early Christian baptistery, and an impressive

Venetian castle. The site's remarkable archaeological discoveries make it an essential destination for history enthusiasts.

The Historic Centre of Gjirokastër:

Another UNESCO World Heritage Site in Albania, the historic center of Gjirokastër, is a well-preserved example of an Ottoman-era town. Its stone houses, narrow cobbled streets, and the imposing Gjirokastër Castle transport visitors back in time. The castle, perched on a hilltop, offers stunning panoramic views of the surrounding area. Exploring Gjirokastër's architecture and heritage provides a glimpse into the region's unique history.

Ottoman and Byzantine Architecture

Ottoman Architecture in Albania:

The Ottoman Empire, which spanned several centuries and encompassed a vast territory, left an indelible mark on Albanian architecture. Ottoman architecture in Albania is characterized by its grandeur, elegance, and synthesis of different architectural elements from diverse cultures.

Mosques: One of the most iconic features of Ottoman architecture in Albania is the presence of magnificent mosques. These structures often boast impressive domes, elegant minarets, and intricately designed facades. The Ethem Bey Mosque in Tirana is a prime example, renowned for its stunning frescoes and ornate decorations.

Bazaars and Caravanserais: Ottoman influence is also evident in the numerous bazaars and caravanserais that dot Albania's cities and towns. These architectural marvels served as vibrant centers of trade, offering shelter and facilities to traveling merchants. The Gjirokastër Bazaar and the Krujë Bazaar are excellent examples that have preserved their Ottoman charm.

Bridges and Fortifications: The Ottomans constructed numerous bridges and fortifications across Albania, essential for communication and defense. The Mostar Bridge in Gjirokastër, characterized by its stone arches and strategic location, is a testament to Ottoman engineering prowess.

Byzantine Architecture in Albania:

Albania's association with Byzantine

architecture is rooted in its historical ties to the Byzantine Empire. Byzantine architecture is known for its ornate decoration, grand mosaics, and iconic domes, reflecting the empire's rich artistic tradition.

Churches and Monasteries: The Byzantine influence is prominently displayed in the numerous churches and monasteries found throughout Albania. These structures exhibit distinct features such as dome-shaped roofs, intricate frescoes, and exquisite iconography. The Church of St. Mary in Berat and the Monastery of St. John Vladimir in Elbasan exemplify the Byzantine architectural style.

Castles and Palaces: Byzantine architecture in Albania is also evident in its castles and palaces, which served as centers of power and defense. The Rozafa Castle in Shkodra, with its commanding position and intricate stonework, exemplifies Byzantine fortification techniques.

Preserving the Heritage:

The preservation and restoration of Ottoman and Byzantine architecture in Albania are crucial for safeguarding the country's cultural identity and attracting tourists. Efforts by the Albanian government, in collaboration with international organizations, have focused on conserving these architectural treasures and promoting sustainable tourism.

Traditional Arts and Crafts

Albanian craftsmanship is characterized by its vibrant colors, meticulous attention to detail, and deep-rooted traditions. These traditional arts and crafts not only showcase the creativity and skills of the Albanian people but also provide a glimpse into the country's history and cultural identity.

Embroidery and Textiles:

One of the most celebrated traditional arts in Albania is embroidery. Embroidery holds a special place in Albanian culture and is often passed down from one generation to another. Skilled artisans create breathtaking designs using vibrant threads, incorporating motifs inspired by nature, mythology, and historical events. Each region in Albania has its unique embroidery style, with distinctive patterns and color combinations. Textiles play a significant role in Albanian folklore, traditional attire, and ceremonial costumes, making them an integral part of the country's cultural heritage.

Woodcarving:

Albanian woodcarving is a time-honored craft that showcases the exceptional skill and artistry of its craftsmen. Woodcarvers transform blocks of wood into intricate masterpieces, ranging from decorative household items to elaborate architectural details. The motifs used in Albanian woodcarving often draw inspiration from nature, folklore, and religious symbols. Furniture adorned with delicate carvings and wooden household utensils exemplify the exquisite craftsmanship and cultural significance of this traditional art form.

Copper and Silver Filigree:

The art of filigree in Albania is a delicate and intricate craft passed down through generations. Skilled artisans meticulously manipulate thin wires of copper or silver into intricate patterns and shapes, creating breathtaking jewelry, decorative objects, and household items. Filigree work often incorporates symbols and designs inspired by Albanian mythology and folklore. The intricate patterns and attention to detail make filigree one of the most cherished traditional arts in Albania, appreciated for its beauty and cultural significance.

Pottery and Ceramics:

Pottery and ceramics have a long-standing tradition in Albania, dating back thousands of years. The country's rich clay deposits provide the raw material for the creation of unique pottery items. Skilled potters shape the clay by hand or using a potter's wheel, creating an array of vessels, plates, and decorative objects. Traditional Albanian pottery is known for its earthy tones, simple yet elegant designs, and often incorporates regional motifs. The craft of pottery not only serves utilitarian purposes but also plays a vital role in preserving Albania's cultural heritage.

Folk Instruments and Musical Crafts:

Albanian traditional arts also encompass musical crafts, with a diverse range of folk instruments representing the country's musical heritage. Instruments like the lahuta (a bowed string instrument), the çifteli (a plucked string instrument), and the zurna (a wind instrument) have been used for centuries to accompany traditional dances and songs.

The craftsmanship involved in creating these instruments demonstrates the skill and dedication of Albanian artisans in preserving their musical traditions.

Preservation and Revival:

While traditional arts and crafts in Albania have faced challenges over time, efforts are being made to preserve and revive these valuable cultural practices. Artisans, cultural organizations, and the government have come together to support traditional craftsmanship through workshops, exhibitions, and educational initiatives. This commitment to preserving traditional arts and crafts ensures that future generations can appreciate and carry forward the cultural legacy of Albania.

Folklore and Music

One of the most vibrant aspects of Albanian culture is its folklore and music. The country's folklore encompasses a wide range of traditional tales, legends, customs, and music that have been passed down through generations, reflecting the history, values, and beliefs of its people. In this guide, we will delve into the captivating world of Albanian folklore and explore the mesmerizing melodies that have captivated audiences for centuries.

Albanian folklore is a tapestry of myths, legends, and oral traditions that have been woven into the fabric of the nation's identity. These stories often revolve around heroes, mythical creatures, and historical events, providing a window into the cultural consciousness of the Albanian people. The tales are replete with themes of love, honor, bravery, and the eternal struggle between good and evil. The epic poem "Gjergj Elez Alia" is a prime example of Albanian folklore, recounting the heroic deeds of its protagonist and embodying the spirit of national pride.

Music is an integral part of Albanian folklore, serving as a medium through which stories are told and emotions are conveyed. Traditional Albanian music is characterized by its distinct melodic patterns, intricate vocal techniques, and unique instruments. One of the most prominent instruments in Albanian folk music is the çifteli, a two-stringed lute-like instrument played with a plectrum. The lahuta, a one-stringed instrument played with a bow, is another significant instrument that adds a hauntingly beautiful element to the music.

Albanian folk music is incredibly diverse, with different regions of the country showcasing their own distinctive styles and rhythms. The northern part of Albania is known for its powerful, polyphonic singing, where multiple voices harmonize to create mesmerizing melodies. The southern regions, on the other hand, boast a more lyrical and melancholic style, often accompanied by dance. The traditional dances of Albania, such as the valle, serve as a visual expression of the music, with their intricate footwork and vibrant costumes captivating audiences.

Throughout history, Albanian folklore and music have played a vital role in preserving the country's cultural heritage and fostering a sense of national identity. During times of occupation and oppression, folk songs and stories served as a form of resistance, allowing the Albanian people to maintain their spirit and pride. Today, folklore festivals and performances continue to be cherished events, where people come together to celebrate their shared traditions and pass them on to future generations.

The fusion of traditional Albanian music with modern influences has also given rise to contemporary genres, such as Albanian folk-pop and folk-rock. These genres combine elements of traditional folk music with modern instruments and arrangements, creating a unique sound that appeals to both younger and older audiences. Artists like Elina Duni and Tirana Jazz Quartet have gained international recognition for their innovative interpretations of Albanian folk music, breathing new life into age-old traditions.

CHAPTER 6

HIDDEN GEMS AND LOCAL SECRETS

Secret Beaches and Coves

There are hidden coastal treasures waiting to be discovered. This guide will take you on a journey to explore the secret beaches and coves in Albania, revealing secluded spots that offer tranquility, natural beauty, and a touch of exclusivity.

Gjipe Beach:

Tucked away between towering cliffs on the southern coast, Gjipe Beach is a true paradise for nature lovers. Accessible only by boat or a thrilling hike, this secluded gem remains unspoiled by mass tourism. Its crystal-clear turquoise waters, pristine sandy beach, and dramatic cliffs make it a perfect hideaway for those seeking serenity and seclusion.

Jale Beach:

Located on the southern Riviera, Jale Beach is a hidden oasis of tranquility. Surrounded by lush vegetation and framed by the dramatic Albanian Alps, this unspoiled stretch of coastline offers a serene and relaxing atmosphere. With its golden sand and crystal-clear waters, Jale Beach is a perfect spot for sunbathing, swimming, and enjoying breathtaking sunsets.

Livadhi Beach:

Nestled on the southwestern coast of Albania, Livadhi Beach is a true hidden gem. This secluded paradise boasts a long stretch of sandy beach flanked by crystal-clear waters and rolling hills. The absence of crowds allows visitors to unwind and immerse themselves in the beauty of the surrounding nature. Enjoy a leisurely swim, indulge in a beachside picnic, or simply relax under the warm Mediterranean sun.

Kakome Bay:

For those who truly seek seclusion, Kakome Bay is an undiscovered haven on the Albanian Riviera. Accessible only by boat or a challenging hike, this pristine cove offers untouched beauty and a sense of exclusivity. Surrounded by rugged cliffs, the secluded beach and turquoise waters of Kakome Bay create an idyllic setting for a private retreat or a romantic escape.

Shën Jani Bay:

Nestled on the picturesque Karaburun Peninsula, Shën Jani Bay enchants visitors with its unspoiled natural beauty. With its pebbled shoreline, clear waters, and breathtaking views of the Adriatic Sea, this hidden gem is a haven for snorkeling, diving, and exploring marine life. Escape the crowds and immerse yourself in the serenity and solitude of Shën Jani Bay.

Grama Bay:

Located on the Albanian Riviera, Grama Bay remains one of the country's best-kept secrets. This remote and secluded beach rewards adventurous travelers with its untouched beauty and tranquil atmosphere. Surrounded by olive groves and lush greenery, Grama Bay offers a secluded retreat where you can unwind, swim in the crystal-clear waters, and marvel at the stunning coastal scenery.

Authentic Local Cuisine

Albania also captivates food enthusiasts with its authentic local cuisine. From hearty meat dishes to fresh seafood delicacies, the Albanian culinary scene offers a delightful array of flavors that will leave your taste buds longing for more. Join us on a gastronomic journey as we explore the authentic local cuisine in Albania and uncover the unique culinary traditions that make this country a true culinary paradise.

The Influence of Geography and History:

Albania's strategic location at the crossroads of Eastern and Western cultures has played a significant role in shaping its cuisine. With a coastline stretching along the Adriatic and Ionian Seas and a landscape characterized by mountains, valleys, and fertile plains, Albania offers a diverse range of ingredients that form the foundation of its gastronomy. Over the centuries, Ottoman, Italian, Greek, and Balkan influences have left their mark on Albanian cuisine, resulting in a captivating fusion of flavors and culinary techniques.

Signature Dishes:

A visit to Albania is incomplete without savoring its signature dishes. One such delight is "Byrek," a savory pastry made with thin layers of filo dough filled with various ingredients such as spinach, cheese, or meat. Byrek is a popular snack enjoyed by locals and visitors alike. Another must-try dish is "Tavë Kosi," a mouthwatering baked lamb and yogurt casserole that perfectly showcases the country's love for tender meats and dairy products. The simplicity of "Fërgesë," a hearty dish made with peppers, tomatoes, and local cheese, is yet another culinary treasure that embodies the essence of Albanian cuisine.

Fresh Seafood Delights:

With its long coastline, Albania is blessed with an abundance of fresh seafood. Coastal cities and towns offer an array of delectable seafood dishes, including grilled fish, octopus salad, and stuffed calamari. "Shkëndija," a traditional coastal seafood stew, is a must-try delicacy that combines a variety of seafood with aromatic herbs and spices, resulting in a harmonious medley of flavors.

The Art of Fermentation:

Albanians have mastered the art of fermentation, which adds depth and complexity to their cuisine. "Kërnacka" and "Dhalle," traditional fermented dairy products, are enjoyed alongside meals and provide a refreshing and tangy contrast. The country's renowned "Raki" deserves a special mention – a potent grape brandy that is not only a popular alcoholic beverage but also an integral part of Albanian cultural traditions.

Regional Specialties:

One of the fascinating aspects of Albanian cuisine is its regional diversity. Each region boasts its own culinary specialties and traditional dishes. In the mountainous north, "Tave Dheu" (lamb and vegetable casserole) and "Kulaç" (a dense cornbread) are popular. In the south, "Qifqi" (rice and meat balls) and "Flija" (layered pancake dish) showcase the culinary treasures of the region. Exploring these regional specialties allows you to immerse yourself in the local traditions and experience the true essence of Albanian gastronomy.

Hidden Mountain Villages

While many visitors flock to the coastal cities and popular tourist destinations, there are hidden gems tucked away in the country's majestic mountains. These hidden mountain villages offer a unique and authentic experience, away from the hustle and bustle of the more well-known areas. In this guide, we will explore some of the most enchanting hidden mountain villages in Albania, where time seems to stand still, and nature's beauty takes center stage.

Theth: Tucked away in the Albanian Alps, Theth is a remote village that exudes charm and natural beauty. Surrounded by towering peaks, Theth is a hiker's paradise, offering breathtaking trails and panoramic views. The village is known for its traditional stone houses with wooden roofs, giving it a rustic and picturesque feel. Visitors can explore the Theth National Park, swim in crystal-clear mountain springs, and witness the renowned "Lock-in Tower," a historic symbol of the village.

Valbona: Nestled in the Valbona Valley National Park, Valbona is a hidden gem that captivates visitors with its untouched wilderness. The village is accessible through a scenic hike or by boat along the crystal-clear Valbona River. Valbona offers a serene atmosphere, with traditional guesthouses providing a cozy retreat for weary travelers. The valley is a paradise for nature enthusiasts, with trails leading to glacial lakes, dense forests, and majestic waterfalls.

Kruja: Located in the heart of the Dajti Mountain range, Kruja is a historic mountain town that transports visitors back in time. The town is famous for its well-preserved Ottoman-era architecture, including the imposing Kruja Castle. History buffs can explore the Skanderbeg Museum, dedicated to Albania's national hero, Gjergj Kastrioti Skanderbeg. Kruja also offers stunning panoramic views of the surrounding mountains and the Adriatic Sea.

Benja: Situated in the rugged terrain of southern Albania, Benja is a hidden gem renowned for its natural hot springs. This mountain village is tucked away in the valley of the Vjosa River and offers a peaceful retreat for those seeking relaxation. Visitors can soak in the therapeutic waters of the thermal baths, surrounded by lush vegetation and cascading waterfalls. The nearby Gjirokastër Fortress, a UNESCO World Heritage Site, is also worth a visit.

Bogë: Perched high in the Albanian Alps, Bogë is a remote village that offers a glimpse into traditional mountain life. The village is surrounded by pristine forests, alpine meadows, and snow-capped peaks, making it a paradise for outdoor enthusiasts. Visitors can embark on hiking adventures, go horseback riding, or simply savor the tranquility of this hidden mountain retreat. The warm hospitality of the locals and the authentic Albanian cuisine further enhance the experience.

Rehova: Tucked away in the Gramoz Mountains near the Greek border, Rehova is a secluded village that enchants visitors with its untouched natural beauty. The village is known for its stone houses, traditional water mills, and breathtaking landscapes. Rehova is an excellent base for exploring the nearby

Lengarica Canyon, where visitors can marvel at its dramatic cliffs and emerald-green river.

CHAPTER 7

TIPS FOR RESPONSIBLE TRAVEL

Respect for Local Customs and Traditions

It is crucial to approach these customs with respect and understanding, as they play a significant role in the lives of Albanians. In this chapter, we will explore the importance of respecting local customs and traditions in Albania, providing insights into the cultural fabric of the country.

Historical Significance:

Albania has a long and complex history influenced by various civilizations, including Illyrians, Romans, Ottomans, and Communism. This diverse historical background has shaped the customs and traditions that are still celebrated today. From traditional music and dance to folklore festivals and religious ceremonies, these customs reflect Albania's rich past and should be regarded with utmost respect. By appreciating the historical significance behind these customs, visitors can gain a deeper understanding of Albanian culture and its people.

Hospitality and Respect:

Albanians are renowned for their warm hospitality and generosity towards guests. When visiting Albania, it is essential to reciprocate this hospitality by showing respect for local customs and traditions. Greetings, for instance, play a vital role in Albanian culture. It is customary to greet others with a firm handshake and direct eye contact. Additionally, addressing elders with proper titles, such as "Zoti" for Mr. and

"Zonja" for Mrs., is considered respectful. By embracing these social norms, visitors can forge meaningful connections with locals and foster positive cultural exchange.

Dress Code:

Albanians take pride in their appearance and often dress formally for special occasions and religious events. When attending such events, it is advisable to dress modestly and avoid revealing clothing. Women may prefer to wear skirts or dresses that cover the knees, while men should opt for long trousers and shirts. By adhering to the local dress code, visitors demonstrate their respect for Albanian traditions and contribute to the overall harmony of the occasion.

Religious Practices:

Religion plays a significant role in Albanian

society, with Islam and Christianity being the predominant faiths. Visitors should respect religious sites, such as mosques and churches, by observing proper etiquette. This may include removing shoes before entering, dressing modestly, and refraining from disruptive behavior. Understanding the importance of these religious sites to the local community allows visitors to demonstrate cultural sensitivity and reverence.

Culinary Traditions:

Albanian cuisine is a delightful blend of Mediterranean, Balkan, and Turkish influences, featuring an array of delicious dishes and regional specialties. When dining with Albanians, it is customary to wait for the host to initiate the meal and to express gratitude for the food by complimenting the cook. Engaging in conversations about traditional cuisine and trying local delicacies not only showcases respect for Albanian customs but also fosters a deeper appreciation for the country's culinary heritage.

Sustainable Tourism Practices

The rapid growth in tourism can often pose challenges to the environment, local communities, and cultural heritage. To mitigate these impacts and ensure the long-term sustainability of the tourism industry, Albania has implemented a range of sustainable tourism practices. This guide explores some of the key initiatives and strategies that have been adopted to promote sustainable tourism in Albania.

Preserving Natural Resources

Albania boasts breathtaking natural beauty, including pristine beaches, rugged mountains, and lush national parks. Recognizing the importance of preserving these valuable resources, the Albanian government has implemented several measures to protect the environment. The establishment and management of protected areas, such as the Albanian Alps National Park and the Butrint National Park, have played a crucial role in conserving biodiversity and promoting sustainable tourism practices. These parks not only protect ecosystems but also provide opportunities for ecotourism, allowing visitors to experience Albania's natural wonders responsibly.

Promoting Community Involvement

Sustainable tourism in Albania emphasizes the involvement of local communities. The concept of community-based tourism has gained momentum, encouraging local residents to actively participate in tourism activities and benefit from them. By engaging communities, tourism initiatives aim to create economic opportunities, empower local residents, and foster a sense of pride in their cultural heritage. Initiatives such as homestays and local tour guide programs enable visitors to interact with local communities, fostering cultural exchange and generating income directly for the residents.

Preserving Cultural Heritage

Albania has a rich historical and cultural heritage, with numerous archaeological sites, Ottoman-era architecture, and traditional crafts. To preserve this heritage, the Albanian government has implemented policies to protect and restore historical landmarks and promote sustainable tourism practices that respect the cultural values of local communities. For example, the city of Gjirokastër, a UNESCO World Heritage site, has implemented conservation and restoration programs to safeguard its unique architectural heritage while offering sustainable tourism experiences. By showcasing and preserving their cultural heritage, local communities can benefit from tourism while maintaining their identity and traditions.

Encouraging Responsible Tourism

To promote responsible and sustainable tourism practices, the Albanian government and various organizations have focused on raising awareness among tourists and industry stakeholders. Initiatives such as the "Leave No Trace" campaign and responsible travel guidelines educate visitors about respecting nature, minimizing waste, and supporting local businesses. Sustainable tourism certifications, like the Green Label, are also being introduced to recognize and promote environmentally friendly accommodation providers and tour operators. By encouraging responsible behavior and supporting sustainable businesses, Albania strives to minimize the negative impact of tourism while maximizing the benefits for local communities and the environment.

Investing in Infrastructure

Infrastructure development plays a crucial role in supporting sustainable tourism practices. Albania has been investing in improving transportation networks, waste management systems, and water and energy infrastructure to accommodate the growing number of tourists without compromising the environment. For instance, sustainable transport options, such as bike-sharing programs and electric vehicle charging stations, are being introduced to reduce carbon emissions. Investments in eco-friendly accommodations, with a focus on energy efficiency and waste reduction, are also on the rise, providing tourists with sustainable lodging options.

Supporting Local Communities

Many communities in Albania face various economic and social challenges. Supporting local communities in Albania is crucial for fostering sustainable development, enhancing livelihoods, and preserving the unique cultural fabric of this remarkable nation. In this guide, we will explore the importance of supporting local communities in Albania and discuss some effective strategies that can be employed to empower these communities.

Importance of Supporting Local Communities:

Economic Growth and Employment Opportunities: Supporting local communities in Albania can stimulate economic growth by promoting entrepreneurship and creating job opportunities. When local businesses thrive, they contribute to the overall economic development of the region. By encouraging local products and services, tourists and visitors can help generate revenue that circulates within the community, leading to greater financial stability for its residents.

Preserving Cultural Heritage: Albania is a country rich in cultural heritage, with distinct traditions, music, dance, and craftsmanship. Supporting local communities ensures the preservation and promotion of these cultural assets. By investing in cultural activities and traditional crafts, local communities can pass on their knowledge and skills to future generations, preserving the unique identity of Albania.

Strengthening Social Cohesion: A strong sense of community fosters social cohesion and unity among the residents of Albania. When local communities are supported, individuals feel a stronger connection to their surroundings and are more likely to engage in activities that benefit the common good. This leads to increased cooperation, social harmony, and a shared sense of responsibility, ultimately contributing to a more inclusive and resilient society.

Effective Strategies for Supporting Local Communities:

Promoting Tourism: Albania boasts breathtaking landscapes, pristine coastlines, and historical sites that attract tourists from around the world. By promoting responsible tourism, visitors can engage with local communities, learn about their customs, and directly contribute to their economic well-being. Encouraging tourists to explore lesser-known regions and participate in community-based tourism initiatives can provide a sustainable source of income for local residents.

Encouraging Local Entrepreneurship: Supporting local entrepreneurs is key to empowering communities in Albania. Governments and organizations can provide financial assistance, training programs, and mentorship opportunities to help aspiring entrepreneurs start and sustain their businesses. Additionally, promoting local products through marketing campaigns and trade fairs can enhance market visibility and create demand for locally made goods.

Investing in Infrastructure and Services: Adequate infrastructure, such as roads, electricity, and healthcare facilities, is crucial for the growth and development of local communities. Governments and NGOs can prioritize investments in infrastructure projects that directly benefit communities, ensuring access to essential services and improving the overall quality of life.

Capacity Building and Education: Education plays a vital role in empowering local communities. Providing access to quality education and vocational training equips individuals with the skills needed to participate in the modern economy. Governments and organizations can establish community centers, workshops, and adult education programs that address specific needs and empower individuals to contribute to their communities effectively.

CHAPTER 8

LANGUAGE GUIDE

Basic Albanian Phrases and Expressions

Albanian, the official language of Albania and Kosovo, is a fascinating Indo-European language with unique features. Learning a few basic Albanian phrases and expressions can greatly enhance your travel experience and help you connect with the locals. In this guide, we will explore essential greetings, useful expressions, and simple conversational phrases in Albanian.

Greetings:

- Tungjatjeta! (Hello!) - A formal way to say "hello" to someone you're meeting for the first time or in a formal setting.

- Pershendetje! (Hi!) - A more informal greeting used among friends and acquaintances.

- Mirëmëngjes! (Good morning!) - Used to greet someone in the morning.

- Mirëdita! (Good day!) - A general greeting used throughout the day.

- Mirëmbrëma! (Good evening!) - Used to greet someone in the evening.

- Natën e mirë! (Good night!) - Used when saying goodbye at night.

Polite Expressions:

- Faleminderit! (Thank you!) - A polite way to express gratitude.

- Ju lutem! (Please/You're welcome!) - Used to politely ask for something or as a response to "thank you."

- Më falni! (Excuse me!) - Used to get someone's attention or when asking for forgiveness.

- Me ndihmoni, ju lutem? (Can you help me, please?) - Useful when seeking assistance.

- Përshëndetje! (Goodbye!) - A formal way to bid farewell.

Basic Conversational Phrases:

- Si jeni? (How are you?) - A common way to ask someone how they are doing.

- Mirë falënderoj, ju lutem. (I'm fine, thank you.) - A typical response to "How are you?"

- Çfarë është emri juaj? (What is your name?) - An expression to ask someone's name.

- Unë quhem... (My name is...) - A way to introduce yourself by stating your name.

- Ku është banjoja? (Where is the restroom?) - A useful phrase when you need to find a restroom.

- Ju lutem flisni më ngadalë. (Please speak more slowly.) - Helpful when someone is speaking too fast for you to understand.

Basic Expressions:

- Po (Yes) and Jo (No) - Simple affirmations or negations.

- Në rend dhe radhë (In line, please) - Used when waiting for your turn.

- Unë nuk kuptoj. (I don't understand.) - A phrase to indicate that you didn't comprehend what was said.

- Më ndihmoni, ju lutem? (Can you help me, please?) - Useful when seeking assistance.

- Çfarë kohë është? (What time is it?) - A

phrase to ask for the time.

Conclusion:

Mastering a few basic Albanian phrases and expressions can significantly enhance your travel experience in Albania and Kosovo. The locals will appreciate your effort to connect with them through their language, and it can open doors to meaningful interactions and cultural experiences. By familiarizing yourself with these essential greetings, polite expressions, and conversational phrases, you'll be well on your way to communicating effectively in Albanian. So go ahead, practice these phrases, and embrace the beauty of the Albanian language during your next visit to this captivating region.

APPENDIX

Useful Websites and Resources

In today's digital age, the internet has become an indispensable tool for accessing information and connecting with people. Albania, a beautiful country nestled in the Balkan Peninsula, has not been left behind in harnessing the power of the web. This guide explores a collection of useful websites and resources in Albania that cater to a wide range of interests and needs. From government portals to travel guides and educational platforms, Albania offers a wealth of online resources to enhance your experience in the country.

Official Government Websites:

Albania's official government websites provide valuable information on various aspects, including travel, business, education, and healthcare. The official government portal (https://www.e-albania.al/) serves as a comprehensive resource for accessing important services, news updates, and official documents. The website offers e-services, allowing individuals and businesses to carry out administrative procedures conveniently.

Visit Albania:

For those planning a visit to Albania, the Visit Albania website (https://www.albania.al/) is an excellent resource. It showcases the country's diverse natural beauty, cultural heritage, and historical landmarks. The website provides information on popular tourist destinations, local events, accommodations, transportation, and travel tips, enabling visitors to plan their trips effectively.

Tirana Times:

Tirana Times (https://www.tiranatimes.com/) is an English-language news portal offering comprehensive coverage of current events, politics, business, culture, and sports in Albania. The website provides timely and reliable news articles, opinion pieces, and analysis, ensuring both locals and foreigners stay informed about the country's latest developments.

Virtual Learning Platforms:

For individuals seeking educational resources, Albania boasts several online learning platforms. Shkolla.al (https://shkolla.al/) is a digital learning platform designed for students and teachers alike. It offers a wide range of educational materials, exercises, and interactive lessons tailored to the Albanian curriculum.

Albanian Telegraphic Agency:

The Albanian Telegraphic Agency (ATA) is a reliable news agency providing both national and international news coverage. The website (https://www.ata.gov.al/) delivers news articles, interviews, and features on politics, economy, culture, and sports. It serves as a valuable resource for those interested in staying up-to-date with the latest news from Albania.

Invest in Albania:

For entrepreneurs and investors considering business opportunities in Albania, Invest in Albania (https://invest-in-albania.org/) is an essential resource. The website offers comprehensive information on investment sectors, legal frameworks, tax incentives, and business regulations. It also provides insights into the country's economic trends and opportunities, assisting prospective investors in making informed decisions.

Albanian Tourism Association:

The Albanian Tourism Association (ATA) website (https://albaniatourism.org/) is a valuable resource for promoting sustainable tourism in the country. It offers information on various tourist destinations, activities, and cultural experiences. Additionally, it provides a platform for local businesses to showcase their services, facilitating connections between tourists and service providers.

Albanian Institute of Science:

The Albanian Institute of Science (https://ais.al/) is an independent research and development organization dedicated to promoting science, innovation, and technology in Albania. The website offers access to research papers, scientific publications, and data analysis reports. It serves as an invaluable resource for researchers, academics, and students interested in exploring the latest advancements in various fields.

Recommended Reading and Films

For those seeking to explore the diverse facets of this enchanting nation, delving into its literature and cinema can provide an immersive and insightful experience. This guide presents a curated list of recommended reading and films that offer a glimpse into Albania's unique culture, history, and society.

Literature:

"Broken April" by Ismail Kadare:

Considered a masterpiece of Albanian literature, this novel explores the intricacies of the Kanun, an ancient code of honor and blood feud. Ismail Kadare's evocative storytelling takes readers on a journey through the rugged Albanian mountains, offering a profound exploration of tradition, violence, and human nature.

"The General of the Dead Army" by Ismail Kadare:

Another remarkable work by Ismail Kadare, this novel reflects on the aftermath of war. It tells the story of an Italian general tasked with exhuming the remains of fallen soldiers from World War II. Through his writing, Kadare reflects on the complexities of memory, loss, and the impact of war on individuals and societies.

"The Siege" by Ismail Kadare:

Set during the Ottoman Empire, "The Siege" delves into the historical Battle of Shkodra. Kadare's gripping narrative explores the clash between the besieging Ottoman forces and the defenders of the fortress, shedding light on the resilience of the Albanian people and their struggle for independence.

"Chronicle in Stone" by Ismail Kadare:

This semi-autobiographical novel vividly captures the author's childhood experiences growing up in the town of Gjirokastër. Through the eyes of a young boy, Kadare depicts the impact of war on a community, while providing a poignant portrayal of the cultural heritage and architectural beauty of Gjirokastër.

"The Palace of Dreams" by Ismail Kadare:

A surreal and thought-provoking novel, "The Palace of Dreams" presents a dystopian society where dreams are collected, analyzed, and controlled. Kadare's allegorical exploration of power, surveillance, and the suppression of individuality offers a captivating read for those interested in philosophical themes.

Films:

"The Forgiveness of Blood" (2011):

Directed by Joshua Marston, this internationally acclaimed drama explores the complexities of blood feuds in modern-day Albania. The film delves into the lives of two teenagers caught in the midst of a feud, shedding light on the profound social and cultural implications of this ancient practice.

"Sworn Virgin" (2015):

Directed by Laura Bispuri, "Sworn Virgin" follows the story of Hana, a young woman who takes an ancient oath to live as a man in order to escape the restrictions imposed on women in traditional Albanian society. The film offers a thought-provoking exploration of gender identity, tradition, and personal freedom.

"The Wedding Ring" (2007):

Directed by Engjëll Jonuzi, this heartwarming film tells the story of a young girl, Rrahje, who embarks on a journey to find a wedding ring for her elder sister. Along the way, Rrahje encounters various characters who embody the diverse cultural traditions of Albania, showcasing the country's vibrant heritage.

"Amnesty" (2011):

Directed by Bujar Alimani, "Amnesty" follows the lives of two immigrants who fall in love in the bustling city of Tirana. The film explores themes of love, identity, and the challenges faced by individuals striving to create a better life for themselves in a rapidly changing society.

Albanian Recipes

Albanian cuisine is a delightful blend of Mediterranean and Balkan flavors that has been shaped by centuries of cultural influences. With its diverse range of ingredients and cooking techniques, Albanian cuisine offers a captivating culinary experience. From hearty meat dishes to fresh seafood delicacies and delectable pastries, Albanian recipes have something to offer for every palate. Join us on a gastronomic journey as we explore the rich flavors and unique dishes that define Albanian cuisine.

Byrek: A Savory Pastry Delight

One cannot discuss Albanian cuisine without mentioning byrek, a savory pastry that is often enjoyed as a breakfast or a snack. Byrek comes in various forms, with the most popular being spinach and cheese byrek. Layers of phyllo dough are filled with a mixture of spinach, feta cheese, and herbs, then baked until golden and crispy. The result is a mouthwatering pastry that is both comforting and satisfying.

Tavë Kosi: A Creamy Lamb and Yogurt Bake

Tavë Kosi is a classic Albanian dish that showcases the country's love for lamb. This hearty casserole combines tender lamb pieces with creamy yogurt, eggs, and a hint of garlic. The dish is baked until the flavors meld together, creating a comforting and flavorful meal. Tavë Kosi is often served with a side of rice or bread and is a staple at Albanian family gatherings and celebrations.

3. Fërgesë: A Cheese and Pepper Delight

Fërgesë is a traditional Albanian dish that

combines the rich flavors of two beloved ingredients: cheese and peppers. Typically made with cottage cheese, roasted red peppers, and a variety of spices, fërgesë is a versatile dish that can be enjoyed as a side or a main course. The combination of creamy cheese and smoky peppers creates a unique and satisfying flavor profile.

Shëndetlie: A Sweet Almond Delicacy

No Albanian meal is complete without a touch of sweetness, and shëndetlie fits the bill perfectly. These small, diamond-shaped cookies are made from ground almonds, sugar, and egg whites. They are delicately flavored with rose water or orange blossom water, giving them a fragrant aroma. Shëndetlie is often served during holidays and special occasions, and they pair perfectly with a cup of Albanian coffee.

Baklava: A Rich Nutty Dessert

Baklava, although not exclusive to Albania, holds a special place in Albanian cuisine. This sweet pastry is made by layering thin sheets of phyllo dough with a mixture of ground nuts, sugar, and spices. Once baked, the baklava is drizzled with a sweet syrup made from honey, lemon juice, and rose water, infusing it with an irresistible sweetness. Baklava is a beloved treat enjoyed by Albanians and is a staple on festive occasions.

Maps and Transportation Guides

To make the most of your journey, it's essential to have reliable maps and transportation guides at your disposal. In this comprehensive guide, we'll explore the importance of maps and transportation guides in Albania and highlight some invaluable resources to enhance your travel experience.

Importance of Maps:

Maps serve as indispensable tools that help travelers navigate their way through unfamiliar territories. In Albania, where roads wind through picturesque mountain ranges, meander along the pristine coastline, and lead to hidden treasures, having an up-to-date map is essential for a seamless and fulfilling journey. By highlighting key landmarks, attractions, and transportation routes, maps provide a sense of direction, enabling travelers to plan their itineraries effectively and discover the country's hidden gems.

Transportation Guides:

Albania boasts an extensive transportation network that offers various options for travelers to explore the country. From bustling cities to quaint villages, from ancient ruins to pristine beaches, getting around Albania is made easier with the help of transportation guides. These guides offer valuable information on public transportation options, including buses, trains, ferries, and rental cars, making it convenient for travelers to choose the mode of transportation that best suits their preferences and needs.

Resources for Maps and Transportation Guides in Albania:

Albania Road Map: The official road map of Albania, available online and at tourist information centers, provides a comprehensive overview of the country's road network. It includes major highways, secondary roads, and points of interest, making it an excellent resource for planning road trips and navigating the country's diverse landscapes.

Mobile Apps: Travelers can download smartphone applications such as Google Maps, Maps.me, and Moovit, which offer detailed maps and real-time navigation features. These apps provide step-by-step directions, estimated travel times, and public transportation information, ensuring a smooth travel experience.

Local Tourism Websites: The official website of the Albanian National Tourism Agency and regional tourism websites provide detailed information on transportation options, including bus and train schedules, ferry services, and car rental agencies. These websites also offer insights into popular tourist destinations, recommended itineraries, and useful travel tips.

Local Guides and Tour Operators: Engaging the services of knowledgeable local guides and tour operators can greatly enhance your travel experience in Albania. These experts have in-depth knowledge of the country's transportation system and can provide valuable insights, personalized recommendations, and even arrange private transportation for specific excursions or tours.

Conclusion:

Maps and transportation guides are indispensable tools for exploring Albania's rich cultural heritage, breathtaking landscapes, and hidden treasures. Whether you're wandering through the ancient streets of Berat, embarking on a road trip along the Albanian Riviera, or venturing into the rugged mountains of the Accursed Peaks, having reliable maps and transportation guides will ensure a seamless and memorable journey. By utilizing the resources mentioned above, you'll be well-equipped to navigate Albania's enchanting landscapes, uncover its hidden gems, and create unforgettable memories along the way. So, grab your map, plan your route, and embark on an extraordinary adventure in the land of the eagles.

Made in the USA
Monee, IL
07 December 2023